JANE AUSTEN

Jane Austen was born in Steventon, Hampshire, in 1775. She
began writing *Pride and Prejudice* in 1796, after staying at
Goodnestone Park in Kent with her brother Edward and his
wife. Originally titled *First Impressions*, it was published by
Thomas Egerton in 1813, anonymously attributed to 'The
Author of *Sense and Sensibility*', her first published novel,
which was sold as having been written 'By a Lady'. It has
become one of the best-loved novels in English literature, and
spawned numerous adaptations, spin-offs, prequels and sequels.
Austen's other novels are *Northanger Abbey*, *Mansfield Park*,
Emma and *Persuasion*. She started work on her seventh novel,
Sanditon, in 1817, but died later that year, having suffered ill
health for some time.

ISOBEL McARTHUR

Isobel McArthur is a Mancunian-Glaswegian actor, director
and playwright. She graduated from the Royal Conservatoire
of Scotland in 2014, and has since performed in and written
for theatres all over the UK, including the Royal Lyceum, the
Citizens, the National Theatre of Scotland and in London's West
End. In addition to the acclaimed *Pride and Prejudice** (**sort
of*), her playwriting credits include an adaptation of *A Christmas
Carol* (Pitlochry Festival Theatre), the one-woman comedy *How
to Sing it* (Tron Theatre), and Daphne Oram's *Wonderful World
of Sound* (Scottish tour). Isobel's plays are also performed in
translation internationally.

Other Adaptations in this Series

ANIMAL FARM
Ian Wooldridge
Adapted from George Orwell

ANNA KARENINA
Helen Edmundson
Adapted from Leo Tolstoy

AROUND THE WORLD IN 80 DAYS
Laura Eason
Adapted from Jules Verne

THE CANTERBURY TALES
Mike Poulton
Adapted from Geoffrey Chaucer

A CHRISTMAS CAROL
Karen Louise Hebden
Adapted from Charles Dickens

CORAM BOY
Helen Edmundson
Adapted from Jamila Gavin

DAVID COPPERFIELD
Alastair Cording
Adapted from Charles Dickens

DIARY OF A NOBODY
Hugh Osborne
Adapted from George Grossmith
& Wheedon Grossmith

DR JEKYLL AND MR HYDE
David Edgar
Adapted from Robert Louis Stevenson

DRACULA: THE BLOODY TRUTH
Le Navet Bete & John Nicholson
Adapted from Bram Stoker

EMMA
Martin Millar and Doon MacKichan
Adapted from Jane Austen

FRANKENSTEIN
Patrick Sandford
Adapted from Mary Shelley

GREAT EXPECTATIONS
Nick Ormerod and Declan Donnellan
Adapted from Charles Dickens

THE HAUNTING
Hugh Janes
Adapted from Charles Dickens

HIS DARK MATERIALS
Nicholas Wright
Adapted from Philip Pullman

THE HOUND OF THE BASKERVILLES
Steven Canny & John Nicholson
Adapted from Arthur Conan Doyle

JANE EYRE
Polly Teale
Adapted from Charlotte Brontë

JEEVES AND WOOSTER IN PERFECT
NONSENSE
The Goodale Brothers
Adapted from P.G. Wodehouse

THE JUNGLE BOOK
Stuart Paterson
Adapted from Rudyard Kipling

KENSUKE'S KINGDOM
Stuart Paterson
Adapted from Michael Morpurgo

KES
Lawrence Till
Adapted from Barry Hines

THE MASSIVE TRAGEDY
OF MADAME BOVARY
John Nicholson & Javier Marzan
Adapted from Gustave Flaubert

NORTHANGER ABBEY
Tim Luscombe
Adapted from Jane Austen

PERSUASION
Mark Healy
Adapted from Jane Austen

THE RAGGED TROUSERED
PHILANTHROPISTS
Howard Brenton
Adapted from Robert Tressell

THE RAILWAY CHILDREN
Mike Kenny
Adapted from E. Nesbit

SENSE AND SENSIBILITY
Mark Healy
Adapted from Jane Austen

SWALLOWS AND AMAZONS
Helen Edmundson and Neil Hannon
Adapted from Arthur Ransome

THE THREE MUSKETEERS
John Nicholson & Le Navet Bete
Adapted from Alexander Dumas

TREASURE ISLAND
Stuart Paterson
Adapted from Robert Louis Stevenson

THE WIND IN THE WILLOWS
Mike Kenny
Adapted from Kenneth Grahame

WHISKY GALORE
Philip Goulding
Adapted from Compton Mackenzie

Isobel McArthur

PRIDE AND PREJUDICE*

(*sort of)

After Jane Austen

NICK HERN BOOKS

London

www.nickhernbooks.co.uk

A Nick Hern Book

Pride and Prejudice* (**sort of*) first published in Great Britain as a paperback original in 2019 by Nick Hern Books Limited, The Glasshouse, 49a Goldhawk Road, London W12 8QP

This revised edition first published in 2021

Pride and Prejudice* (**sort of*) copyright © 2019, 2021 Isobel McArthur

Isobel McArthur has asserted her right to be identified as the author of this work

Cover illustration by Bob Venables; design by Muse Creative

Designed and typeset by Nick Hern Books, London
Printed in Great Britain by 4Edge, Essex

A CIP catalogue record for this book is available from the British Library

ISBN 978 1 83904 046 7

Introduction
Isobel McArthur

On the Origins and Spirit of the Show

Pride and Prejudice* (**sort of*) was first performed at the Tron
Theatre in Glasgow in 2018. I suspect that it is the inherent
humour and heart of Glaswegian audiences which initially
imbued this text with the flare, wit and generosity of spirit that I
hope are still at the core of it. It should feel affectionate-whilst-
knowing, front-footed, funny, fourth-wall-breaking and utterly
celebratory.

On Music

In the original production, songs were sung over specially
composed karaoke backing tracks, with some live
instrumentation performed by the actors.

Whilst designed to be performed by five actor-musicians,
the show need not necessarily demand instrumentation or
professionally trained singers. As with delivery of any karaoke
performance, passion is the most essential ingredient.

On Multirolling

This is an adaptation that adores its source text. However, a
further layer of reality and humour presents itself because of
multirolling and the pace of that in live performance. The joke
that we are all in on (that there are only just enough pairs of
hands to pull this off) forms a big part of the overall presentation
of *Pride and Prejudice** (**sort of*) – and much of an audience's
enjoyment can be derived from seeing which performer will
pop up next, and as which character, if they will make their

costumes change in time for their next entrance, etc. There is a
sense of impressive resourcefulness in seeing five actors play
all the parts – in a way that speaks to the circumstances of many
of the women in Jane Austen's novels – but that also amuses
audiences and stretches performers. This means that some of
the characters can be worn lightly and, in many moments, the
personality of the actor can shine through. I would encourage
anyone approaching the text to experiment with these elements
in production.

On Accent and Dialect

Parts of this script were written with specific actors in mind.
Where many period dramas are dominated by received
pronunciation (RP), our original ensemble drew on their own
regional-accent diversity to build the characters, meaning we
heard voices from Glasgow, Newry, Aberdeen, Manchester,
West Yorkshire, Edinburgh and more. There are many words
which sit better in different mouths ('wee', 'mard-arse', etc.),
and which are ways of speaking particular to these different
regions. Anyone performing the show should feel free to alter
these words to something which suits the natural voice of the
performer in each case.

On Casting

I'm sure we all know just how important it is to create more
opportunities for female performers to play a wide range of
nuanced, interesting and varied roles in the theatre. However,
there are also many artistic reasons why an all-female cast
is so perfect for the telling of this particular story. *Pride and
Prejudice* is about the plight of five daughters. Their future
hangs in the balance because none of them were born male. So,
at its very heart, this was always a woman's story.

However, the book is also set during the Napoleonic Wars
(something less frequently touched on in adaptations), meaning
a disproportionate amount of household servants were women

at the time. Indeed, fines were imposed for hiring male servants who might otherwise be usefully employed as soldiers. It seemed crucial that a story so tied up in class and societal status (and one which, itself, has been afforded such a lofty degree of cultural capital) was told by servants. But it also made historical sense for these servants to be women. This way, we watch five women embody their employers, including those who are men, in an act of doubly transgressive triumph.

Jane Austen could not publish under her own name during her lifetime because of her gender. I'm lucky enough to live in a time when I can put my name – and hers – on the front of this book and we, as a company, are all so grateful to her for writing this brilliant story.

Pride and Prejudice* (*sort of) was first performed at the Tron Theatre, Glasgow, on 29 June 2018, produced by Tron Theatre Company and Blood of the Young. The play was subsequently revived on tour of the UK in 2019, produced by the Royal Lyceum Theatre Edinburgh, Tron Theatre Company and Blood of the Young, with co-producers Birmingham Repertory Theatre, Bristol Old Vic, Leeds Playhouse, Northern Stage, Nuffield Southampton Theatres and Oxford Playhouse. The cast was as follows:

TORI BURGESS
FELIXE FORDE
CHRISTINA GORDON
HANNAH JARRETT-SCOTT
ISOBEL MCARTHUR
MEGHAN TYLER

Director	Paul Brotherston
Designer	Ana Inés Jabares-Pita
Musical Supervisor	MJ McCarthy
Lighting Designer	Simon Hayes
Sound Designer	MJ McCarthy
Choreographer	EJ Boyle
Associate Director	Shilpa T-Hyland
Dramaturgy	Johnny McKnight
Associate Designer	Anna Orton
Associate Sound Designer	Calum Paterson
Casting Director	Laura Donnelly CDG (Additional Casting)

Pride and Prejudice* (*sort of) transferred to the Criterion
Theatre, London, on 2 November 2021 (previews from 15
October), with David Pugh presenting Tron Theatre Company,
the Royal Lyceum Theatre Edinburgh and Blood of the Young's
production (original direction by Paul Brotherston), with co-
producers Birmingham Repertory Theatre, Bristol Old Vic,
Leeds Playhouse, Northern Stage and Oxford Playhouse. The
cast was as follows:

TORI BURGESS
CHRISTINA GORDON
HANNAH JARRETT-SCOTT
ISOBEL MCARTHUR
MEGHAN TYLER

Understudies
ANNABEL BALDWIN
LEAH JAMIESON

Directors	Isobel McArthur and Simon Harvey
Comedy Staging	Jos Houben
Designer	Ana Inés Jabares-Pita
Lighting Designer	Colin Grenfell
Musical Supervisor	Michael John McCarthy
Sound Designer	Michael John McCarthy
	and Luke Swaffield for Autograph
Choreographer	Emily Jane Boyle
Casting Director	Sarah Bird
Company Manager	Mark Vince
Deputy Stage Manager	Jackie Ellis
Assistant Stage Managers	Jodie Day and Lizzy Gethings
Wardrobe Mistress	Megan Keegan
Sound Operator	Maisie Roberts

PRIDE AND PREJUDICE[*]

(*sort of)

Isobel McArthur
after Jane Austen

Characters

SERVANTS

A phalanx of housekeepers, chambermaids, cooks and other servant staff from Miss Austen's novels.
They transcend all worlds, all times and steer the course of the action in ways unnoticed by the master characters.
They include…

ANNE
TILLIE
CLARA
FLO
EFFIE

…all of whom play the servants of any household, as required.

MASTERS

MRS BENNET, *mother to five unmarried daughters*
MR BENNET, *her husband (played by a chair)*
JANE BENNET, *the eldest Bennet daughter. Beautiful*
ELIZABETH BENNET, *the second-eldest Bennet daughter.*
    Our heroine
MARY BENNET, *the middle Bennet child. A social outcast.*
    Nervous, bookish. A certain kind of intelligent
KITTY BENNET, *the second-youngest Bennet daughter. Never*
    seen. Competes with Lydia
LYDIA BENNET, *the youngest Bennet at fifteen. Precocious*
MR COLLINS, *their cousin. A slimy clergyman*
CHARLOTTE LUCAS, *best friend to Elizabeth*
CHARLES BINGLEY, *a rich, single young man. Extremely*
    affable
MISS CAROLINE BINGLEY, *his insufferably snobby sister*

FITZWILLIAM DARCY, *another rich, single young man. Best
    friends with Bingley. Reserved. Prone to negativity*
GEORGE WICKHAM, *a very charming and handsome soldier*
LADY CATHERINE DE BOURGH, *Darcy's incredibly rich aunt*
MRS GARDINER, *aunt to the Bennet girls. Likeable, caring*

Multirolling

ACTOR 1 – Flo, Mrs Bennet, Fitzwilliam Darcy
ACTOR 2 – Tillie, Charlotte Lucas, Charles Bingley,
    Miss Bingley
ACTOR 3 – Effie, Elizabeth Bennet
ACTOR 4 – Clara, Jane Bennet, George Wickham, Lady
    Catherine de Bourgh
ACTOR 5 – Anne, Mary Bennet, Lydia Bennet, Mr Collins,
    Mrs Gardiner

Multirolling can get complicated. Fast costume changes and
strong characterisation from a talented multirolling cast will
be necessary to maintain clarity and pace throughout.

Music

The piece features karaoke songs, usually sung over a backing
track. There will occasionally be live instrumentation – largely
played by the servants. Incidental/textural/atmospheric sound is
also used to tell the story.

Text

Should generally go at a right lick.

Note on Text

Lines sung or spoken on microphones appear in **bold**. (This
script suggests a convention of speaking letters on microphones
– but this can be experimented with.)

A forward slash (/) indicates the point at which the following line of dialogue overlaps.

Decoding the Names of Some Domestic Locations

Longbourn – *the Bennets' house*

Netherfield – *the house Charles Bingley rents in Meryton*

The Parsonage – *Mr Collins' house*

Rosings – *Lady Catherine's house*

Pemberley – *Darcy's house*

This text went to press before the end of rehearsals and so may differ slightly from the play as performed.

ACT ONE

Pre-Show

As the audience arrive, we can hear servants' bells ringing. Five
SERVANTS *in Regency-era dress emerge from a small door*
'below stairs'. Cries of 'coming' as bells ring and they leave
and re-enter the stage.

There are books strewn everywhere, and the SERVANTS *must*
dust the bookshelves and tidy them all away. They push a piano
into the space for dusting.

A chandelier is hoisted down by one SERVANT *so another can*
dust it. The height is repeatedly misjudged by the absent-minded
hoister who sends the chandelier higher and higher, so that the
dusting SERVANT *must climb the stairs to get at it. It is*
increasingly precarious with the hoister eventually getting
distracted by a ringing bell and letting the rope go altogether!
The chandelier falls through the air, about to smash on the floor
– when another SERVANT *catches the rope at the last minute.*
The chandelier is saved, but the action has sent the SERVANT
into the side of the bookcase, from which all the carefully
arranged books now fall, making a mess. They are back to
square one.

Music will be needed to boost morale.

Scene One – Prologue

One SERVANT *begins to sing – an opening song – Elvis*
Costello and the Attractions' 'Everyday I Write the Book' with a
cry of –

TILLIE. Good evening!

> – *at the top of the instrumental.*

> *The song concludes.*

> *The books are cleared away.*

> *They address the audience. They are welcoming, polite – but playful, too.* EFFIE *is exhausted and sits apart.*

TILLIE. Alright?

CLARA. Now! You've all come to enjoy Miss Austen's famous story –

ANNE. We know – we've been expecting you.

TILLIE (*looking at the audience's expressions*). But maybe yous weren't expecting us?

FLO. Or, you were expecting us to pop in now and then –

TILLIE. At the tinkle of a bell –

CLARA. Serve the tea –

ANNE. And then piss off.

FLO. To make room for the *main characters*.

CLARA. In all Miss Austen's great novels there are masters –

TILLE. And there are servants.

CLARA. Romantic heroes –

TILLIE. and brief cameos.

CLARA. And whilst some go about their lives of leisure searching for love –

TILLIE (*holding one*). Others, empty pishy chamberpots.

CLARA. But know this: servants are integral to love stories.

ANNE. You try having a whirlwind romance without –

TILLIE. Clean bedding.

ANNE. And, you know what else – (*Conspiratorial.*) the smallest action can change the whole story.

CLARA (*also conspiring*). Think about it – *we* pull the strings. *We* actually make it happen.

FLO. By delivering a letter that bit slower or topping up a glass that bit quicker – !

ANNE. Before you know it – the lovers are walking off arm-in-arm into the sunset –

TILLIE. All thanks to us.

A collective sigh of satisfaction.

CLARA (*less convinced*). It's such satisfying work. Seeing them all happy like that. And knowing that we did our bit.

Beat. Strained smiles.

FLO. Shame about the wee… oversight on Miss Austen's part.

ANNE. You see there's –

TILLIE. No ever-after for us.

CLARA. No love interests. And –

EFFIE (*forlorn*). No ending.

They turn and look at EFFIE. *They mustn't give in to sadness.*

FLO (*unconvincingly*). Still – it's reassuring to have job security –

TILLIE. For all eternity.

ANNE. And they say servants who work hard are never short of true friends.

Energy. Sharing smiles. They'll do it for each other.

CLARA. So! You may not have spotted the servants – but rest assured, we were always there –

TILLIE. Ready –

FLO. Primed –

CLARA. Waiting for the bell to ring.

TILLIE. We have been doing this since 1796.

FLO. Nothing shocks us – !

ANNE. We are always dependable –

CLARA. In fact – indispensable!

TILLIE (*a warning to the audience*). And you, masters of households shouldn't forget, we've seen everyone –

ANNE. Absolutely everyone –

ALL. Naked.

Beat. They look at the audience.

CLARA. So, now that we all 'know our place'…?

TILLIE *takes a green piece of costume over to* EFFIE. EFFIE *looks up and smiles for the first time. She takes it.*

FLO. Let's begin!

Everyone moves to their beginners' places.

Scene Two

Everyone leaps into action – a colossal Regency dressing screen placed to establish 'Longbourn' as the SERVANTS *address the audience.*

CLARA. The story starts here. A sleepy wee place, about halfway between London and Cambridge, called – Meryton.

ANNE. There's a bit of a problem with emotional repression here.

FLO. So don't be surprised if people burst into song every now and again.

ANNE. For the ladies, in particular, there's very little to do.

CLARA. So they're reliant on a steady import of gossip to help pass the time. Luckily, this week brought the exciting news that the landlord of Netherfield Park has finally found a tenant!

All running on gossip like fuel – !

FLO. One *Charles Bingley*. And he's not local.

CLARA. No – this man is new! Just moved to the area –

ANNE. And not only is he rich enough to rent a place like Netherfield –

FLO. With a fortune to live off besides –

CLARA. He's also young, handsome and *single*.

ANNE. Tonight is the monthly town ball! A chance for all the locals to meet this new wealthy resident.

CLARA. Just as well – Meryton is home to many unmarried ladies. And it is a truth universally acknowledged that a single man, in possession of a good fortune, *must* be in want of a wife.

All at once lights change, the SERVANTS *disappear, noises of a scrap and* MRS BENNET *is spat out from behind the screen.*

MRS BENNET. I give up! You are all impossible! (*Ringing a bell.*) Tillie!

TILLIE *enters.*

TILLIE (*to the audience*). Welcome! This Meryton household is known as Longbourn. And it is home to the Bennet family.

MRS BENNET. *Tillie!*

TILLIE. Coming! (*To audience.*) This is my mistress, Mrs Bennet. Mother to five unmarried daughters.

MRS BENNET. Help the girls on with their dresses, Tillie, or we'll be late. Oh, it's too much pressure… (*Sucking on her inhaler.*)

TILLIE *tightens the bodice of someone behind the dressing screen and addresses the audience.*

TILLIE. She's a wee bit tense. You see, if the girls don't have husbands when their da dies, they'll all be destitute. Mrs Bennet included. Because in Regency-era England, women can't inherit money or property.

A yelp from behind the screen.

– Just breathe in a little, miss – I know that's all changed since, but you can understand the logic at the time. *Spinsters* don't need material things, do they? No coal for the fire? Probably having a nice hot flush. Hungry? Just eat one of the cats that surround them in such huge numbers. As for money? Ach, they'd only spend it on romance novels and Cinzano.

So these girls will automatically lose their home, their belongings and every penny in the bank unless one of them marries a man who can inherit it for them.

MRS BENNET. Jane! Let me look at you.

JANE emerges and does a reluctant twirl.

You are an angel! Do you see, girls, how pleasing she is?

A sarcastic sound of agreement from the crowd behind the screen.

This Mr Bingley won't be able to take his eyes off you.

JANE. Mum…

MRS BENNET. Is she not a vision?

ELIZABETH appears.

ELIZABETH. *Jane* would look nice if we lacquered her in liquid shite. *Jane's* not a cause for concern…

MRS BENNET. Elizabeth Bennet!

ELIZABETH (*to* JANE). We should be asking, 'Will Mr Bingley be good enough for *you*?'

JANE. He might not like me. Maybe he'll prefer you! Imagine, Lizzie, if he was your soulmate – and from this night forward you were safe, secure and happy for the rest of your life.

ELIZABETH. Meh. I could take it or leave it.

MRS BENNET. Elizabeth! I'm trusting you to keep your conversation... easy this evening. In fact, I'm not trusting you – let him do the talking.

ELIZABETH. But men *hate* to dominate conversations, don't they?

MRS BENNET. Being a fucking smart-arse, Lizzie... (*Remembering herself.*) is not ladylike.

TILLIE (*appearing*). So you've got the eldest, Jane – the beautiful one (inside and out). And Liz, the sarky one. Loyal sisters, those two.

MRS BENNET. You'd all do well to listen to my advice! Didn't I marry a gentleman?

ELIZABETH. Where is Dad?

MRS BENNET. Where do you think? Sat in that bloody chair, smoking his pipe... (*Seeing someone behind the screen.*) Jesus, Lydia! Put them away!

LYDIA. But everyone says I have a really sexy pair of (*Emerging, skirt hoisted an inch.*) ankles.

MRS BENNET (*scandalised*). We are not running a brothel!

TILLIE (*lacing* LYDIA's *shoes*). Lydia's the baby. Only fifteen. Attention-seeking wee bam who just does not give a shi–

LYDIA. Did you say something, Tillie?

TILLIE. Oh, no, miss.

LYDIA (*threateningly*). Good.

MRS BENNET. Now, Kitty!

Silence.

Kitty, have you chosen a dress?

A growl of frustration. From behind the screen, a dress is thrown. It hits LYDIA.

LYDIA. This is mine, you thieving bitch!

LYDIA *runs behind the screen. She and* KITTY *have a physical fight behind it which we hear parts of. The screen shakes,* TILLIE *steadies it.*

TILLIE (*to audience*). Kitty's almost one year older than Lydia. But it's hard to say if she's any wiser. Who am I missing? Oh yes, Mary. The middle child. Easily forgotten. To give her her dues, she's… studious. But you wouldn't want to spend time with her or anything.

MRS BENNET. Mary – ? (*Seeing her emerge.*) Lord in Heaven, can anything be done…?

MARY *has obviously made a big effort to dress up – but the clothes are wearing her. It is the most ridiculous, unattractive, over-the-top attempt at femininity. Pink satin, bows, frou-frou, flowers, puffball sleeves.*

MARY (*emboldened*). I've been thinking about it. The financial situation. I've read every book in the house. Maybe I could tutor part-time. That way we could –

MRS BENNET. Hush, Mary – that's an awful lot of talking. Now, smile as you will when you meet Mr Bingley.

MARY *attempts this. It's awful.*

Why don't you try looking shy?

This is even worse. Out of despair, TILLIE *exits up the stairs.*

Well, it's not all about looks, is it?

MARY. I could sing.

ALL. No!

MRS BENNET. How many times, Mary? Think of my nerves! You must *never* sing in public. Especially if there are eligible men in attendance.

MARY. But why?

MRS BENNET. I've made it very clear why! (*Puts an arm around her – whispers.*) You are *too good*. You make the others look bad. Yours is a talent that's best... kept hidden. Okay?

MARY *nods. Some other girls giggle.*

Girls, focus! You will not be the only single women at this ball. Mrs Long has unmarried nieces and you know she's a crafty cow... Mrs Lucas still has Charlotte to marry off – she's no spring chicken –

ELIZABETH. Charlotte's a friend, Mum –

MRS BENNET. Not tonight, Liz! *Tonight* she's your direct competition. The Lucases are good-looking in that very obvious way. Sadly some men don't appreciate... (*Looking at her motley assembly of daughters.*) ...nuance. But whatever this Bingley chap is into, we need to identify it. (*Moving to* JANE.) He might want someone beautiful, Jane (*Moving to* ELIZABETH.) – or someone spirited, Liz! (*Faced with* MARY.) or someone... else, Mary. But you must *all* smile! Charm! Dance! Sing! – No, not you – and who knows, by the end of the evening we may just have secured our future. Now, you know your positions. Go! Go! Go! Go! Go!

The space transforms.

Scene Three

Lights! A really crappy party. Kylie Minogue's 'I Should Be So Lucky'. TILLIE is on the high stairs, dancing. She addresses the audience.

TILLIE (*to someone in front row*). How do you feel about balls, folks?

CLARA (*entering with a trolly of drinks*). Because here in
    Meryton –

    TILLIE *releases a sign from up high 'The Meryton Town
    Ball'*.

    If you're not talking about the last town ball –

TILLIE. Or talking about the next town ball –

CLARA. It's because you're at the current town ball.
    And because they're public events – (*Eyeing* LYDIA
    approaching.) *anyone* can get in…

    CLARA *lifts a tray of drinks from the trolly.* LYDIA *takes
    one and* CLARA *turns to go* –

LYDIA. Ah-ah! Hold on. Give it us. (*Taking the whole tray.*)
    What? I've got four sisters. We dehydrate easily! (*Exits.*)

ELIZABETH (*despairing*). Lydia! One of these days…

MRS BENNET (*entering*). Elizabeth! Keep an eye out for Mr
    Bingley!

ELIZABETH. I am, Mum!

CLARA. Whatever your view on balls, they're great for seeing
    pals. And Elizabeth's best friend – apart from her sisters, of
    course – was always Charlotte Lucas.

    CHARLOTTE *enters from upstage. She spots* ELIZABETH.
    CHARLOTTE *stops, gazes at her, neatens her hair, takes a
    breath – then makes the approach.*

CHARLOTTE. Liz!

ELIZABETH. Charlotte! I'm so glad you're here! (*Looking
    around the room.*)

CHARLOTTE. Aw, really?

ELIZABETH. You can help me find this Charles Bingley guy.

CHARLOTTE (*disappointed*). Oh, well I've not seen him yet.

ELIZABETH. They're saying he's young, free, minted and
    good-looking. So what the fuck is he doing in Meryton?

CHARLOTTE. My mum says there's actually two of them. Charles Bingley is bringing his sister –

ELIZABETH. Well, I can't marry a woman!

CHARLOTTE. Well... no. I meant, he's bringing his sister *and* his best friend – Fitzwilliam Darcy. He's single, too. In fact, they say he's even richer than Bingley.

ELIZABETH. So our odds have doubled!

CHARLOTTE. Well, your odds were always high, Liz. (*Softly.*) Everyone falls for you in the end.

ELIZABETH *laughs*. CHARLOTTE *remembers herself*.

But I suppose love's irrelevant – we're talking about marriage.

ELIZABETH *whirrs around to see* CHARLOTTE, *but she has gone and been replaced with* MARY *who is dancing*. MRS BENNET *spots her*.

MRS BENNET. Oh for God's sake, Mary, are you hell-bent on sabotage? Stop it! Have you seen him yet?

MARY *shakes her head*.

CLARA (*to audience*). Little did Mrs Bennet know, Charles Bingley had already arrived.

BINGLEY (*entering*). I never want it to end! I've decided – I'll throw the next ball! At my place! A month is far too long to wait for another!

BINGLEY *struggles to remove his right hand from a Pringle tube it has become stuck inside*.

CLARA. He was nice to look at, unpretentious, and so at ease with everyone – the perfect gentleman.

MRS BENNET. Oh my God. That must be him! Go and fetch Jane!

MARY *exits*.

MRS BENNET (*trying to put on the airs*). Mr Bingley! Sir! What a pleasure it is to finally meet you. I am Mrs Bennet.

BINGLEY. Oh, yes! Lovely! Lovely! (*Putting out the be-Pringle-tubed hand for Mrs Bennet to shake.*)

MRS BENNET. You must meet my daughters! (*Looks around for them – sees* MARY *reentering.*) Not you, Mary! Are you mad? Get Jane!

MARY *disappears again.*

MRS BENNET (*to* BINGLEY). You will have heard them mentioned, no doubt, by others? They are all very fondly regarded, my girls!

Beat. No sign of JANE.

May I enquire as to how your journey was, sir? No difficulties, I trust, in getting here?

BINGLEY. Getting here? No, no. In fact, in the end, we got here!

MRS BENNET (*laughing far too much*). I'm so pleased to hear it. (*Looking for* JANE, *seeing no one – then buying time with more laughter.*)

JANE *enters.*

Finally! Jane, this is Charles Bingley.

BINGLEY *turns at the sound of his name and sees* JANE *for the first time.* MRS BENNET *throws some confetti and intensely romantic music starts to play – Consuelo Velázquez's 'Bésame Mucho'.* JANE *and* BINGLEY *are both enthralled.* MRS BENNET *remains central, ruining the moment at intervals.* LYDIA *has come through the curtain and is watching.*

Smile, Jane.

She does.

Beat.

Swoosh your dress a little.

She does.

Beat.

I have to tell you, Mr Bingley, she's a wonderful dancer. (*To* JANE.) Dance, Jane, dance!

She does. LYDIA *runs over to* BINGLEY. *The lights revert back – the romantic bubble is burst.*

LYDIA. Mr Bingley, *I* can fit my whole fist in my mouth. Look – !

MRS BENNET. Lydia! Ignore her, Mr Bingley. (*Marching* LYDIA *away.*) Jane, why don't you sing for him? She has a beautiful voice.

BINGLEY. I'm sure.

MRS BENNET (*to* LYDIA). No more drink!

JANE. Mum...!

The backing starts.

MRS BENNET. Oh look, it's started now – so you might as well. (*Pushes* JANE *forward.*)

The Shirelles' 'Will You Still Love Me Tomorrow?' JANE *begins alone – eventually* BINGLEY *joins in and it becomes his question to her as well.* MRS BENNET *exits in pursuit of* LYDIA. *During the instrumental –*

BINGLEY (*a bit too quietly*). God, I'd love to kiss you...

JANE (*not hearing*). What?

BINGLEY. Uh, I said – can I get you a drink?

JANE. Oh, please!

He goes. ELIZABETH *enters the room and watches loved-up* JANE *sing. Two* SERVANTS *join on backing vocals. The song concludes.*

MRS BENNET *re-enters.*

ELIZABETH. Look at her, Mum. Smitten. Like that.

MRS BENNET. I knew he'd like Jane! Mr Bingley is quite the gentleman... Have you seen the sister? Caroline Bingley? (*Rubbing her fingers and thumb together.*) *Lovely* clothes!

MRS BENNET *points as* MISS BINGLEY *enters – as described, she looks wealthy. She seems dissatisfied with everyone and is followed by* ANNE *who is offering out snacks.*

ANNE (*offering*). Can I interest madam in a Wagon Wheel?

MISS BINGLEY (*as if this should be obvious*). No.

JANE. Miss Bingley! (*Running over to her.*) What a pleasure to be able to meet Charles's sister.

MISS BINGLEY. You are?

JANE. Jane Bennet.

MISS BINGLEY. Ah. I hear you and my brother have been 'singing'?

JANE. ...yes.

A beat. MISS BINGLEY *looks* JANE *up and down. She's nowhere near good enough.*

MISS BINGLEY. I've decided that you are going to spend the evening with me.

JANE. Oh, am I?

MISS BINGLEY. Of course. I couldn't possibly allow him to keep such an... interesting creature all to himself now, could I?

JANE. It would be my pleasure to sp–

MISS BINGLEY. Yes, it probably would. (*Turning to leave with* JANE.)

ANNE (*offering* JANE). Miss?

MISS BINGLEY. No!

MISS BINGLEY *knocks the tray out of* ANNE's *hands and drags* JANE *away with her. The Wagon Wheels are all over the floor.* ANNE *clears them.*

ELIZABETH. To think that a brother and sister could be so different.

MRS BENNET. I know!

Beat.

They look nothing alike. (*Sighing to herself.*) Finally, a bit of class. Right, I'm off for a piss.

MRS BENNET *leaves.* BINGLEY *enters with two drinks.*

BINGLEY. Jane?

ELIZABETH. I'm afraid she's just been stolen by your sister. I'm *her* sister, by the way. Elizabeth.

ELIZABETH *offers a hand to shake.* BINGLEY *realises he cannot do this with two drinks, so hands them both to her, only to find this is no better.*

BINGLEY. The final Bennet sister! Now I know Jane, and the lovely Kitty and Lydia – or was it Lydia then Kitty…? And, erm… Mavis?

ELIZABETH. Close enough.

ANNE *passes with an absurd pineapple hedgehog.*
DARCY *appears on the high balcony, looking beleaguered.*
ELIZABETH *takes some cheese from the 'hog.*

BINGLEY (*to himself*). Ooh! Pineapple hedgehog. (*Calling up.*) Darcy! Darcy?

DARCY *pretends not to hear.*

In a world of his own! Do excuse me.

BINGLEY *runs up to* DARCY. ELIZABETH *enjoys her cheese.*

ANNE. Mr Darcy's entrance had drawn the attention of the entire room. He looked good. He looked… rich. But, pretty soon, there wasn't a single guest who didn't wish the mard-arse would just bugger off. (*Exiting.*)

DARCY. Get me out of here. I don't know how you do it. These aren't your people, Bingley, any more than they're mine. Toothless farmers' daughters throwing themselves at me left right and centre.

BINGLEY. Well, Jane Bennet's beautiful, isn't she?

DARCY. She's passable.

BINGLEY. Why not introduce yourself to one of the others?

DARCY *glances around.* ELIZABETH *directly in his eyeline.*

DARCY. There's no one here I'm even remotely interested in.

JANE *re-enters and goes to join her sister. They whisper and gossip.*

BINGLEY (*seeing the karaoke machine*). I've got an idea! You get a drink. If I can't show you a good time in the next ten minutes, we'll leave – I promise.

DARCY. Fine. Ten minutes.

ELIZABETH *and* JANE *burst out laughing – a huge, carefree cackle.*

(*Shuddering at the sound.*) You know who I can't stand?

BINGLEY. Who?

DARCY. People.

BINGLEY. You really are a miserable old fart.

JANE *and* DARCY *both move off and almost bump into each other.*

JANE (*with a small curtsy*). Good evening.

DARCY. Is it? Don't let me keep you.

JANE. Sorry?

DARCY. My friend, Bingley. I dare say you're stalking him.

JANE (*extremely embarrassed*). Charles Bingley? I mean – what? Is that even who you were – ? Is Charles even his first – ? 'Cause I didn't. I barely – Did you mean? 'Cause he's not even really my type!

Beat.

DARCY (*reading her very badly*). In that case, I apologise. I was obviously quite mistaken.

DARCY *leaves, chewing in this.* JANE *cringes.* BINGLEY *indicates* ELIZABETH *toying with a microphone.*

BINGLEY. Jane! Looks like your sister's singing. Are you dancing?

JANE. You asking?

BINGLEY. 'Me asking'?

JANE. Yeah. Are you?

BINGLEY. Am I what?

JANE. Asking.

BINGLEY. Asking?

JANE. Asking me.

BINGLEY. Like a question, you mean, or – ?

JANE (*baffled*). What?

BINGLEY (*not having heard*). What?

JANE. Whether I'll – (*She takes a different tack.*) I'll dance with you, Bingley, if you're up for it?

BINGLEY. Oh, great, yes please. Perfect – your sister shall sing and we shall dance to it! Finishing touches then… Elizabeth – I will fetch you both a singing partner and a captive audience. Jane – I'll be right back!

He dashes off. The two eldest sisters watch him go – then are finally alone.

ELIZABETH. Oh my God!

JANE. I know!

ELIZABETH. I approve!

JANE. I can't believe it. I love him. I think I actually love him. (*Wide-eyed.*) I've heard folk talk about this feeling. I've read about it, of course. But I always assumed, if we were going to survive, that *I'd* never have that... *love*-love. 'Cause I'd have to marry... whoever. But, the thought that I could have both... (*Tearing up.*) I just didn't think this would be my story. Oh, everyone should be able to feel like this!

ELIZABETH *puts her arm round* JANE.

ELIZABETH. You deserve happiness more than anyone.

JANE. Why?

ELIZABETH. 'Cause only you talk about love like that.

JANE. And his sister just invited me to lunch at theirs next week!

ELIZABETH. Perfect!

JANE. Do you think he likes me?

ELIZABETH. Nah. He's obviously just using you to get into Mum's pants.

BINGLEY *re-enters with* MARY *and* DARCY. *The sisters collect themselves.*

BINGLEY. Right, as promised, Mary will be our audience –

MARY. Or I could sing with – ?

JANE/ELIZABETH. No.

BINGLEY. And, he may not be perfect, but he'll do for a duet! Ladies and... ladies – Mr Fitzwilliam Darcy!

Enthusiastic applause. BINGLEY *holds the second mic out to his friend.* DARCY *looks up from a book he's taken to reading.*

DARCY. No, I won't be doing that.

BINGLEY. Go on! We'd love to hear you.

All overlapping.

MARY. / Yes, please, Mr Darcy, it would give everyone such pleasure!

JANE. / I hear you're very good!

ELIZABETH. / Don't force him. You don't have to, Mr Darcy.

BINGLEY. / Come on, you big idiot! Everyone else has had a go.

DARCY. I really would rather not. I'm not a singer.

DARCY approaches BINGLEY to bring a stop to this all. This is misinterpreted as compliance. All cheer.

MARY. / Yes! How wonderful, he's coming up.

BINGLEY. / That's the spirit mate, I knew you'd come around!

The music plays. The opening bars of Marvin Gaye and Kim Weston's 'It Takes Two'. The women dance and enthuse beneath this.

DARCY (*to BINGLEY*). What do you think you're doing? You know I don't sing!

BINGLEY (*to everyone on the mic*). **Here he is!**

DARCY (*low, to BINGLEY*). Sing the bloody song yourself!

BINGLEY (*to DARCY*). I want to dance with Jane – (*Playfully – into the mic.*) **Don't be scared, the beautiful Elizabeth will be by your side!**

Cheering – the song has begun.

ELIZABETH *sings the song.*

BINGLEY (*demonstrating, takes the next line*). Come on, Darcy – !

DARCY. What are you playing at – ?

BINGLEY. Darcy!

DARCY. Are you mad – ?

BINGLEY. Come on now –

DARCY. Why would I waste another moment at this barn dance?

BINGLEY. Darcy – !

The women tune into DARCY, *the mic now directed at his mouth by* BINGLEY.

DARCY. You'd have me paired with the plainest woman in the entire room just to entertain her *idiotic family*?!

Gasps. All chatter out. ELIZABETH *decidedly switches off the karaoke track. All eyes on* DARCY. *Shocked silence.*

Stillness.

A couple of beats.

MARY. Should have let me sing it.

JANE. Mary!

BINGLEY. Mate...

DARCY (*stiffly*). Excuse me... I don't perform to strangers.

BINGLEY. Elizabeth, I am so sorry –

ELIZABETH *is shaking. Doubled over.*

JANE. Are you okay? Don't worry about singing, Lizzie.

BINGLEY. Yes – (*Raising his hand.*) My fault, I shouldn't have pressurised anybody.

We now see she's laughing. A lot.

JANE. Liz?

ELIZABETH. Mic, please.

The backing comes in. Carly Simon's 'You're So Vain'. DARCY *is fixed to the spot.*

I'd like to dedicate this song to a very special someone.

ELIZABETH *sings the first verse and chorus.* DARCY *is drawn to* ELIZABETH, *equally furious and beguiled. The others watch until the echo of 'You're so vain', when they join in, rip off their costumes and transform the space.*

The sound of the music changes – duller now, as if we're hearing it through a wall.

Scene Four

And we are. We're in the 'loos' at the Meryton ball. On one side, the gents' with DARCY *and* BINGLEY. *On the other, the ladies' with* ELIZABETH.

DARCY (*drying his hands*). Can we please leave?

BINGLEY (*clutching his stomach*). Might need to give me a minute, mate. Bloody Scotch eggs... (*Disappearing behind the screen.*)

DARCY (*preening in the mirror*). The last thing that I am is vain. 'Vanity' is a preoccupation with what other people think of you. 'Pride' concerns how you think of yourself. You'd think someone as intelligent as Elizabeth would know the difference. Don't get me wrong, she's not at all...! But those eyes. Well, they're clearly intelligent eyes.

Beat.

Are you coming out then?

BINGLEY *groans from behind the cubicle door.*

Honestly, that man's bowels... (*Shouting to* BINGLEY.) I'll wait for you in the carriage! (*Exiting.*)

Lights down on the gents'. CHARLOTTE *emerges from behind the screen in the ladies'.*

ELIZABETH. Did you see Jane and Bingley?

CHARLOTTE. Jane should start dropping hints about marriage.

ELIZABETH. Steady on, she should get to know him first...!

CHARLOTTE. No! Bingley could have his pick of the women. Jane should show twice as much affection as she feels –

ELIZABETH. Bullshit.

CHARLOTTE. – And marry him as soon as possible. There'll be plenty of time for falling in love later.

ELIZABETH. You don't really think Jane should just throw herself at him?

CHARLOTTE. Well, we all need husbands.

ELIZABETH. Forget about husbands – you're telling me, if you had feelings for someone, you'd just come right out and say it.

CHARLOTTE. It depends. If you were close. (*Moving close to* ELIZABETH.) Knew each other's secrets… understood each other really well…

ELIZABETH (*gently fixing* CHARLOTTE*'s hair*). I'd still need them to make the first move, I think.

CHARLOTTE.…really?

> CHARLOTTE *looks at her intensely – she considers kissing her.*

ELIZABETH. But Jane and Bingley aren't like that anyway. They've only just met.

CHARLOTTE (*pulling away, hurt – she misread this*). If Jane married him tomorrow she'd have as much chance of happiness as she would if she'd studied him for ten years. It's always a gamble. In fact, the less you know about the man's faults, the better.

ELIZABETH. That's mad! What about – what's it called – 'love'!

CHARLOTTE. Wake up, Liz. You could be out on the street tomorrow.

ELIZABETH. You sound like my mother. She's sour 'cause she's been ignored by her husband for a decade. (*Playfully putting her arms around* CHARLOTTE.) But what's your excuse?

CHARLOTTE. Can't say.

ELIZABETH. I think someone needs to get in touch with their cold heart. (*Kisses her on the cheek*.) And that's coming from me! See you out there.

ELIZABETH *leaves.* CHARLOTTE *touches her cheek and watches her go. We can hear the music from the adjoining room, more clearly now, The Divine Comedy's 'Everybody Knows (Except You)'.* ANNE *can now be seen, in marigolds, handing* CHARLOTTE *a microphone.* CHARLOTTE *sings and on the final line, she can make out* ELIZABETH *passing in the scene transition.*

The song concludes. The scene has transformed. ANNE *gives* CHARLOTTE *toilet paper to dab her eyes.*

Scene Five

Longbourn – the same bedroom with dressing screen. The family fuss over JANE.

ANNE (*to audience – spraying a little air freshener to disappear the previous scene*). The day eventually came for Jane to visit the illustrious Netherfield Park and take lunch with Charles Bingley and his houseguests.

MRS BENNET. Oh no, it's a disaster! (*Ringing bell.*) Tillie!

JANE. What?

MRS BENNET. We have a tear! And in your best dress, Jane! Mr Bingley will think she's feral – the whole enterprise is doomed! (*Inhaler.*)

TILLIE *enters, dutifully falls to her knees and takes to mending* JANE's *dress.*

JANE. It'll be okay.

MRS BENNET. You must make the very most of every opportunity to compliment him!

LYDIA. Snog him!

ELIZABETH. Just have fun! If Caroline Bingley doesn't suck all the life out of it.

JANE. She's always been lovely to me.

ELIZABETH. I don't trust her.

JANE (*struggling to speak as* LYDIA *applies lipstick*). Schum people… awre just nice.

ELIZABETH. No they are not. Just don't let her take advantage of your good nature.

MRS BENNET. Let her take a bit of advantage, if it helps matters. And let him take anything he wants. Apart from… You know. (*Amused.*) He mustn't take *that* 'til the wedding night.

ELIZABETH/LYDIA/JANE. Mum…!

LYDIA. Eugh! I'm gonna vom.

TILLIE. All fixed, madam.

MRS BENNET. Show me – (*Gesturing for* JANE *to twirl.*)

The dress is fixed.

Thank God! Now – go outside and mount Willie.

A beat.

JANE. Do what?

MRS BENNET. Get on Willie! He's all ready for you.

JANE. I'm going there on horseback?

ELIZABETH. There's a perfectly good carriage she can ride in.

MRS BENNET. The carriage isn't free.

TILLIE/JANE/LYDIA/ELIZABETH. Yes it is.

Beat. MRS BENNET *feels the eyes on her.*

MRS BENNET. Look – it's going to rain at exactly two o'clock today. So, if Jane goes now, she will have a perfectly pleasant dry ride on Willie –

It's too much for LYDIA *who is in stitches.*

Then, just as they are finishing lunch, the heavens will open and – oh no! Poor Jane will be forced to spend an extra hour with Mr Bingley – because it's raining and she has no carriage with her.

ELIZABETH. Mum! That's...

LYDIA. Brilliant.

MRS BENNET. I'm not canvassing opinion, it's what you're doing. Now, hurry up! You've got a long way to go!

Music swells. Willie is brought onto stage.

Longbourn disappears. Now JANE *is astride a life-size horse. She sings Etta James's 'At Last'.*

Over the first verse, JANE *and Willie enjoy the shining of the sun and twittering of the birds in this suspiciously idyllic English countryside. The* SERVANTS *provide sound effects, birdlife and after a moment or two – a couple of drops of rain.* JANE *feels this but puts on a smile and keeps singing.*

Some winds really pick up. JANE *copes as well as she can, still trying to enjoy her journey and keep her hair neat.*

Then –

Torrential rainfall, thunder, dark skies, high winds, impossible conditions. Willie and JANE *battle on, barely coping, the song has become unrecognisable. It has all gone disastrously wrong. As the chaos peaks,* JANE *is deserted, we lose sight of her and Willie. The weather continues to make a racket and the scene transforms.*

Scene Six

Longbourn. The Bennet's living room. Dusk. MR BENNET's chair faces upstage as usual. MARY, ELIZABETH and MRS BENNET sit. Tension. The clock ticks. MRS BENNET feels the eyes on her.

Beat.

MRS BENNET. Well, you can shut up for a start, Mary.

It will have been one of those rich meals. Where you have to sit and digest for a *long* time afterwards. Then you need to eat something sweet to put you right.

Buns!

A vast choice of buns, probably.

Silence.

It's just more time for Jane to make a good account of herself. Unless it went so badly that she's too ashamed to come home. Oh I knew it – we'll have nothing! We'll all starve!

ELIZABETH. Everything will be fine. Although it did absolutely piss it down the moment she left.

MRS BENNET. Total exaggeration! A little rain never hurt anyone. Did it, Mr Bennet?

Everyone looks at the chair.

He says nothing.

The clock ticks.

MARY *takes out a book.*

Beat.

MARY *clears her throat, turns a page.*

Beat.

MARY *makes a barely audible noise of interest.*

(*Exploding.*) What is the meaning of this incessant *rustling,* Mary?! For heaven's sake! You never showed any discretion in your rustlage. Rustle any more and you'll create a through-draft! And then your father will catch a chill! And when a man his age catches a chill, it's only a matter of time before he – (*Overwhelmed, looking back at the chair, at the thought of* MR BENNET*'s death.*) – oh God, why couldn't I have had sons?

TILLIE *enters holding a letter.*

TILLIE. Miss – ? (*Approaching* ELIZABETH.)

MRS BENNET. What? What is it?

ELIZABETH (*reading*). It's a letter from Netherfield.

Everyone leans in.

Jane got there but she's unwell.

MRS BENNET. Fantastic!

ELIZABETH. They're putting her up until she's recovered.

MRS BENNET. Yes!

MARY. I suppose you'd be pleased, would you, Mother, if her head fell off as well? Then you could relax in the knowledge that it was all in pursuit of a rich man.

ELIZABETH. Look! (*Handing over the letter.*)

MARY. Mother?

MRS BENNET (*studying the letter*). Grown-ups talking, Mary.

ELIZABETH. I should be with Jane.

MRS BENNET. Lizzie, it doesn't say that she's *very* ill.

ELIZABETH. I need to.

MARY. It's still raining, Liz.

ELIZABETH (*unconvincingly*). Be nice to get out. Fresh air.

MRS BENNET. All of the horses are needed on the farm – there's none spare for transport.

ELIZABETH. I'll manage!

MARY. But Netherfield is three-point-two miles, or five-point-one-four kilometres away!

ELIZABETH. I'm going! Tillie?

TILLIE *helps her on with her coat. The scene transforms.* ELIZABETH *becomes aware of quite how heavy the rain is.*

Scene Seven

Netherfield – fancier than what we're used to. A gaudy vase on a plinth, an opulently upholstered chaise longue on which lounges MISS BINGLEY. *She clicks her fingers impatiently at a* HARPIST *who begins to play for her.* ANNE, *a servant appears.*

ANNE (*to audience*). Welcome to Netherfield Park! It's a bit posher than the last place.

There is knocking at the door.

MISS BINGLEY. Someone answer the door!

ANNE. Master Bingley's hired me whilst he's renting here. (*Taking in* MISS BINGLEY.) And of course, his sister's here, making a holiday out of it.

Knocking.

MISS BINGLEY (*to* ANNE). Where've you been? Can't you hear that? Answer it!

ANNE. She's a little ray of sunshine. Even Mr Darcy's staying a little longer. He'll be somewhere with his nose in book…

More knocking at the door.

So it is three-times the linen for me – but then I'm once, twice, three-times a laundry-maid. Coming! (*Exiting.*) 'And I love, you-oo…'

Loud banging at the door – it stops suddenly. ELIZABETH *enters unselfconsciously, mud on her skirts right up to her thighs, she is covered in nature. Flushed, breathless, sweaty.* ANNE *in tow.*

ELIZABETH. I'm here to see my sister.

Astonishment at this figure in the doorway. The HARPIST *has fallen silent.*

Please?

MISS BINGLEY. Elizabeth Bennet? What on earth are you doing?

ELIZABETH. Jane is sick. I've come to be with her.

MISS BINGLEY. On foot? Alone?

ELIZABETH. Yes. Where is she?

MISS BINGLEY. But, the state of you! You're traipsing mud all through the house. You can't expect to stay here.

DARCY *is on the stairs.*

DARCY. Miss Elizabeth!

ELIZABETH. Ah, Mr Darcy.

MISS BINGLEY. Look at her, Darcy! Look at the floor!

ELIZABETH. Sorry to disturb you all, but I really would like to see my sister.

Beat. He looks at her. Astounded.

Through here, is she?

ELIZABETH *exits, walking mud all through the house to* MISS BINGLEY's *horror.* ANNE *rushes to clean it up.* DARCY *whispers something in* ANNE's *ear –* ANNE *stops cleaning and leaves instead.*

MISS BINGLEY. Who does she think she is? It's perverse!
Letting herself get into that state and then turning up
unannounced – ?!

DARCY. She must have been desperate.

MISS BINGLEY. Well yes, it –

The HARPIST *attempts to re-start the song.*

No harp!

The HARPIST *exits.*

(*To* DARCY.) It is a form of desperation, I suppose. The only
way she can get attention. I literally thought a stray dog had
wandered in there.

DARCY. Bingley will have to invite her to stay too. She can't
go back out in this weather.

MISS BINGLEY (*floundering*). Well… yes, if having her to stay
were practical. But, unfortunately, the staff aren't prepared –

ANNE *re-enters cheerily.*

ANNE (*entering*). All done, Mr Darcy! Master Bingley's
delighted. I've made up an extra bed, I've set another place
at the table and a boy's been sent to let the Bennets know that
Miss Elizabeth will be with us for the duration.

MISS BINGLEY. But –

ANNE. Master Bingley's delighted.

DARCY. This is very charitable of you and Bingley, Caroline.

MISS BINGLEY (*through gritted teeth*). Thank you. I'm sure
we'll all have a very pleasant evening together.

DARCY. Perhaps several pleasant evenings if poor Jane doesn't
improve.

He exits.

MISS BINGLEY (*kicking* ANNE). You! Call for the doctor
again! Let's not have the Bennets here any longer than we
need to.

ANNE *smiles and nods dutifully – but there is the twinkle of personal victory in her eye.*

Embarkation on a period of four days.

Scene Eight

ANNE. But no one was going anywhere. Jane was still really under the weather and Elizabeth could only avoid the other houseguests for so long…

DARCY *is at the chaise with a pack of cards.* ELIZABETH *nearby.* MISS BINGLEY *narrows her eyes and stares at her.*

DARCY. Miss Elizabeth – Will you join in a game of cards?

ELIZABETH. Thank you. I think I'll just read.

DARCY. Please – (*Gesturing for her to sit next to him.*)

ELIZABETH *sits on the edge of the chaise, back to him, and reads.*

Beat.

MISS BINGLEY. So you prefer books… to games?

ELIZABETH. Sometimes.

DARCY. Eminently sensible.

MISS BINGLEY. Yes, yes. I am a vorrowcious reader myself.

DARCY. Really?

MISS BINGLEY. Yes! You know that. I am appalled at how tiny the library here is.

Not like your library at Pemberley, Darcy. You won't have seen Mr Darcy's library at his home in Derbyshire, Elizabeth, because – well, why would you? But I can tell you from experience… it's *huge*.

ELIZABETH. Right. (*Returning to her book.*)

MISS BINGLEY *forces herself into the small space between* DARCY *and* ELIZABETH. *Begrudgingly,* DARCY *deals himself and* MISS BINGLEY *some cards.*

MISS BINGLEY. What am I doing here, Darcy, when I could be in that nice big house? If I lived in a home like yours, I could bring all my things, couldn't I? Here, there's only room for one or two trifles. (*Indicating the vase.*) Like this, Miss Elizabeth, do you like it?

DARCY *plays a card.*

ELIZABETH (*not looking*). It's beautiful.

MISS BINGLEY. No, no – over here. It was my housewarming gift to Charles. Japanese. Incredibly rare. I don't imagine you'll have seen anything like it before. Seems out of place in Meryton. Some things should just never leave London.

MISS BINGLEY *plays a card.*

I do miss your little sister, Darcy! How is the sweet girl?

DARCY. Not so little. About the same height as… Miss Elizabeth, by now.

DARCY *plays a card.*

MISS BINGLEY (*irritated*). Yes, yes – but *she's* so accomplished, isn't she? Young Georgiana.

MISS BINGLEY *picks up a card.* DARCY *plays a card.*

ELIZABETH. What makes a woman 'accomplished', then?

MISS BINGLEY. You need to know all about fashion, play an instrument, sing, draw and dance to a very high standard. You need to speak a foreign language – one of the nice ones – walk gracefully, come from a respectable family and look really, really nice all the time. And then *maybe* you'll be halfway there.

MISS BINGLEY *picks up a card.*

DARCY. And, most importantly, she must read.

DARCY *plays a card*.

I rarely meet truly accomplished women. Maybe six in my entire life.

MISS BINGLEY. Yes, exactly, me too.

ELIZABETH. I have never met *anyone* who can claim to do all those things.

MISS BINGLEY. Maybe you haven't, Miss Elizabeth, but Mr Darcy and I know a hundred such women.

MISS BINGLEY *plays a card*.

ELIZABETH. A hundred? The six women from earlier have multiplied at an impressive rate. But, then, they are high achievers. (*Looking at the last card played*.) Oh, I think someone's failed to follow suit.

MISS BINGLEY (*picking up her misplayed card – eyeing* ELIZABETH). Thank you. I was impressed enough at your first accolade of the weekend: 'Walker of Long Distances' – but to think that we can add 'Reader of Books' *and* 'Keen Referee of Games She's Not Even Playing'.

Quite amazing.

ELIZABETH. I might check on Jane, excuse me.

ELIZABETH *leaves*.

MISS BINGLEY. Well, if there were ever any doubt.

DARCY. Of?

MISS BINGLEY. She's one of those women who hates all women. Doing down womankind in order to make herself more attractive to men. It's pathetic behaviour, don't you think, Mr Darcy?

DARCY. Absolutely. Pathetic.

DARCY *plays his final card. He has won*.

MISS BINGLEY. Oh. Well done you.

ELIZABETH (*re-entering*). Asleep.

DARCY *sits to write a letter.* MISS BINGLEY *spreads herself across the entire chaise leaving no room for* ELIZABETH. ELIZABETH *takes a chair to sit with her book –* DARCY *cannot help but watch her.* MISS BINGLEY *sees this and picks up a book herself, mirroring* ELIZABETH *– her book upside down. She looks to see if* DARCY*'s watching – but he has returned to writing his letter.* MISS BINGLEY *tosses the book over her shoulder and walks into the middle of the room, humming, then singing a bit to herself. She begins to dance. She tries to be really sexy and interesting right in* DARCY*'s eyeline trying various poses and moves in her attempt at seduction.*

MISS BINGLEY. Elizabeth! Seeing me dance like this… you probably want to come and join me?

ELIZABETH. Not especially. There isn't any musi–

MISS BINGLEY *grabs her and drags her to the spot.*

MISS BINGLEY. There! Now we're two friends, dancing together, side by side.

MISS BINGLEY *dances absurdly in the silence, occasionally holding hands with or throwing her arm around* ELIZABETH *as if they were great mates.* ELIZABETH *tries to appease her, joining in but knowing it's bizarre.*

(*To* ELIZABETH.) Let's see your signature move.

ELIZABETH. My what?

MISS BINGLEY *does her own signature move.*

MISS BINGLEY (*shouting to* DARCY). Do you like the dance, Darcy? Share your thoughts.

DARCY. Please assume I am consistently impressed.

MISS BINGLEY. Well, then you'll join us in a dance, won't you?

DARCY. No.

MISS BINGLEY. Why ever not?

DARCY. There are only two reasons you could be stood there pretending to dance. Either you are gossiping about me –

ELIZABETH. I assure you that's not the case.

DARCY. – In which case, I'd better stay out of earshot. Or *else,* you want me to *admire you* as you dance –

MISS BINGLEY. Mr Darcy!

DARCY. – In which case, I'd better stay here where I can get a good view.

MISS BINGLEY. Shocking! Shocking!

Oooh, isn't he cheeky?! However shall we punish him?

ANNE *enters.*

ANNE. Miss Bingley – I beg your pardon but Jane is awake and asking for you.

MISS BINGLEY. For me? Not Elizabeth?

ANNE. She considers you a dear friend for taking her in, miss. I could send up Master Bingley instead? (*Cheekily.*) I'm sure he'd love to pop up to her bedroom and give her a good –

MISS BINGLEY. *No!* …No. I shall go.

She looks furious that she has to leave these two together, smiles falsely and leaves.

DARCY *and* ELIZABETH *see each other.*

It is the first time they've ever been alone.

The HARPIST *has appeared. They play a delicate instrumental arrangement of Pulp's 'Something Changed'.*

ANNE (*softly*). As the days passed, Elizabeth could not help noticing how often his eyes were fixed on her. For a man who hated her company, he was behaving very strangely. She didn't like him very much. Well, not enough to ask what that look really meant.

For Darcy, the division of feeling surprised him. And he wasn't a big fan of surprises. He had let himself spend too much time with her. He resolved to avoid Elizabeth altogether until her sister was well and they both were gone.

DARCY *turns to face away.* ELIZABETH *exits confused. Music fades.*

MISS BINGLEY *enters.*

MISS BINGLEY. What a relief they're almost ready to leave. Four days ago I'd have described Elizabeth Bennet as a minor irritation. Now I find her mere presence positively unsettling. Do you not agree, Darcy?

DARCY. I do.

The scene transforms.

Scene Nine

JANE *wheeling luggage on, arriving home.* MR BENNET *in his chair, as always.* LYDIA *is holding a knitting needle.*

Apart, a large suitcase in the middle of the space.

LYDIA (*to the house*). Kitty! Kitty! Where are you? You said you'd let me pierce your ears! Mum? Mum!

MRS BENNET *enters with an inhaler and a cigarette on the go, shouting to* KITTY *who is off.*

MRS BENNET. Oh Kitty, just let her give your ears a bit of a pierce. (*Seeing* JANE *and* ELIZABETH.) Thank God you're back! You've been missed. So – did he propose?

ELIZABETH (*embarrassed*). Propose? Why on earth would he – ? He's just some rude egotist who we barely know.

MRS BENNET. Nonsense! Charles Bingley's the most cheerful man you could meet.

ELIZABETH. Oh. Yes. Bingley.

MRS BENNET. Who on earth are you talking about?

JANE. No, Mum. Of course he didn't propose to me, I was bed-ridden for the whole stay.

MRS BENNET. Useless! We're cursed. Elizabeth – you at least sold yourself to Miss Bingley as sister-in-law material?

Beat. She looks at them.

If you can't tell me good things, girls, just lie to me!

In unison, both non-committal.

ELIZABETH. / We're the best of friends. It was an absolute hoot. No worries.

JANE. Everyone got on really well while I was upstairs coughing, yes.

MRS BENNET. Good.

ELIZABETH *sees the suitcase.*

ELIZABETH. Whose is this?

MRS BENNET. Yes... Your father's cousin, Mr Collins, is here.

TILLIE (*to audience*). The girls have never met William Collins before. Oh – and neither have you! Savour this moment. You don't know how bloody lucky you are.

Collins is Mr Bennet's only living male relative. In other words, if the girls remain unmarried, it's him who'll inherit the lot. The house. The furniture. The good sherry. The mould on the cream cheese... Even me.

MRS BENNET. The day may come when Mr Collins can do with us as he wishes. So we all need to welcome him warmly. Even if he is a bit of a –

The sound of a toilet flushing, off. COLLINS *enters.*

Mr Collins! (*Leaping up.*) Can I present the two young ladies you haven't yet met: Jane and Elizabeth.

COLLINS (*staring at the ceiling*). Those light fixtures would have to go...

MRS BENNET. Um, Mr Collins – may I introduce you?

COLLINS. Oh – (*To* JANE.) Elizabeth, is it?

JANE. Jane, actually.

COLLINS (*turning to* ELIZABETH). And?

MRS BENNET. Well, Elizabeth.

COLLINS. I have to say, Mrs Bennet – they are fairly elegant. I mean, not as elegant as Lady Catherine and her daughter.

MRS BENNET. No. Of course.

ELIZABETH. Who's Lady Catherine?

COLLINS. *Who*? *The* Lady Catherine of Rosings, of course. My patroness. And my neighbour. A woman of unmatched class, fortune, taste, condescension –

MRS BENNET. She has been very kind to Mr Collins. Thanks to her he is a clergyman with his own parish and a lovely home.

COLLINS. Yes, she has made me very comfortable. And I have seen the inside of her home... eight times.

ELIZABETH (*sarcastically*). Wow.

COLLINS (*to* MRS BENNET). You see, Mrs Bennet – I am a natural with women. And strangely, apart from Lady Catherine – did I mention? Lady Catherine? She's my patroness – apart from her, I actually know very few women.

(*To* JANE.) Lovely smile. And your teeth are the same colour as the skirting. Seems silly to break up a set.

JANE *looks horrified*.

MRS BENNET. A... set? (*Her eyes widen as she understands*.)

MRS BENNET *moves in front of* MR COLLINS *and pretends to cry unconvincingly.* MR COLLINS *looks at her.*

Oh I am sorry, Mr Collins – I was just thinking of my poor girls and how they'll all be destitute –

COLLINS. Well, Mrs Bennet, funnily enough I intend to prevent that.

MRS BENNET. You do?! How exactly –

COLLINS. I promise to have a look at all of your girls… (*Taking in the room again.*) …needs replastering… to see if any of them are suitable. For me. Wife-wise.

MRS BENNET. Oh – Mr Collins, you would be the saviour of this family! If I might have a discreet word… Jane is engaged. Virtually. There's a gentleman, Charles Bingley, and we're expecting the proposal any day now.

COLLINS. Jane?

MRS BENNET (*demonstrably*). The one in blue is not available. But… perhaps as you get to know them all this week one of the others might eventually seem acceptable to you?

Scene Ten

MRS BENNET, JANE, ELIZABETH *and* MR BENNET *host* MR COLLINS. *They are all bored to tears.* MRS BENNET *sits attentively listening, or trying to look like she's listening, everyone else is practically falling asleep whilst* MR COLLINS *talks. And talks.*

TILLIE. Mr Collins stayed for what felt like months. He was not a sensible man.

COLLINS.…indistinguishable in shape from a new potato…

TILLIE. Everything that genetics had failed to give him –

COLLINS. Pus. Everywhere.

TILLIE. Education and life experience had also failed to give him. So the interval of waiting appeared very, very long before he said:

COLLINS. Mrs Bennet, I wondered if I might speak to that one in private?

Beat.

Then – chaos! MRS BENNET *flies out of her seat. Voices overlapping. All very fast.*

MRS BENNET. Of course, Mr Collins! / Tillie, move my husband!

JANE (*smirking*). / Oh my God…

ELIZABETH. / Mum, no – !

TILLIE *begins to wheel* MR BENNET *off the stage.*

MRS BENNET. / Jane! In here! (*Opening a small cupboard to shove* JANE *into.*)

TILLIE. / Come on, sir.

JANE (*looking into the cupboard*). It's very dark.

MRS BENNET. Crouch, Jane! / Move him, Tillie!

ELIZABETH. / Please!

MRS BENNET (*grabbing an escaping* ELIZABETH). Lizzie, show our guest some courtesy! (*To* TILLIE *and* JANE.) I said get out!

Bang. All doors shut. All noise out. The light in the space is reduced to a small pool. COLLINS *and* ELIZABETH *alone.*

COLLINS. Pretending you don't want to be left alone with me. I find that very endearing.

ELIZABETH (*despairing*). Oh, Mr Collins –

COLLINS. Oh, Jane.

Beat.

I mean: Oh, Elizabeth.

ELIZABETH. No, I wasn't swooning –

COLLINS. Please, let me speak. I know we're both worried about being overcome with passion… So, to keep things formal. (*He takes out a piece of paper.*) I've prepared a list of reasons why we should marry.

ELIZABETH. There really is no need for that.

COLLINS (*surprised*). Oh! Well, I heard young ladies were eager these days – but you are chomping at the bit, aren't you?

ELIZABETH. No, I –

COLLINS. Say no more! I'll do away with this and let you have your moment tout de suite! (*Attempting to kneel.*)

ELIZABETH. No, you don't need to –

COLLINS. You're right, I'll just stand. Now, miss…?

He pauses. She can't understand why. Then realises –

ELIZABETH. Elizabeth!

COLLINS. Elizabeth – that's it, Elizabeth, Elizabeth, Elizabeth – will you give me your hand in marriage?

ELIZABETH. Thank you. But I'm going to say 'no'.

COLLINS. I see. I know that for appearance's sake, some ladies like to refuse a man a couple of times before saying yes.

ELIZABETH. Sorry, which ladies –

COLLINS. So for the second time, will you marry me?

ELIZABETH. Why do you think this is a come-on?

COLLINS. Well, you'd never refuse. You'd have to be mad. Comfortable life, save your family from financial ruin and – hello – you get me. But I don't mind playing along if you'd like to create some more suspense.

ELIZABETH. Get that idea out of your head! I am not some coy creature toying with you. I am a rational person saying 'no'. How can I make this clearer?

Eager as ever, he holds out the ring for a third proposal.

Fuck off.

COLLINS *face drops. She means it – and he can't believe it.*

COLLINS. Mrs Bennet – !

MRS BENNET (*sticking head out with balloons and a tooter*). Congratulations!

ELIZABETH. What?

MRS BENNET. Sorry, you first.

JANE *also emerges from the cupboard.*

ELIZABETH. I said 'no'.

MRS BENNET. This is a joke?

ELIZABETH. No. I don't want to marry him. So I said no.

MRS BENNET (*horrified*). Tillie! Fetch Mr Bennet! (*To* ELIZABETH.) Just you wait – !

TILLIE *wheels* MR BENNET *back on.*

Liz, do you see what you're doing? Breaking my heart, disappointing poor Mr Collins –

COLLINS. I'm happy to ask a fourth time but –

MRS BENNET. And your sisters! Think of their future! You wouldn't hurt your family like that, would you?

ELIZABETH. I just can't.

MRS BENNET. Tell her, Mr Bennet! Tell her if she doesn't marry him, we will never speak to her again.

Beat.

(*To* ELIZABETH.) I am serious.

ELIZABETH. Then I suppose you will never speak to me again.

MRS BENNET *can't believe it.*

COLLINS. Excuse me. I think I will… take the air.

TILLIE. There's a lovely clear path on the left that'll take you just past the Lucas's house, sir.

COLLINS *leaves.*

MRS BENNET. God knows if we'll ever see him again, the way he's been treated!

TILLIE. Beg your pardon, madam, but you'll surely be taking him along this evening? To the ball Mr Bingley is hosting?

MRS BENNET. Oh good God, the Netherfield Ball – that's tonight! Jane – go! You need to look amazing. And you prep the carriage, Tillie!

JANE *and* TILLIE *exit*.

(*To* ELIZABETH.) You will dance with Collins all evening – won't she, Mr Bennet? – Tell her.

Silence. MRS BENNET *looks at the chair*.

Just a few words from you at this point could make a big difference to the lives of your daughters.

Silence.

Lizzie always listens to you. She worships you.

Silence.

Come on, I don't ask you for much.

Silence.

(*Defeated – taking in her daughter and husband*.) You are both unfathomable to me.

MRS BENNET *leaves*. ELIZABETH *sighs. She mouths the words 'Thank you' at her father*.

MISS BINGLEY *appears in an enormous, ludicrous Ascot-style hat. She is holding a rehoboam of champagne which she drinks through a crazy straw as she shouts into the wing*.

MISS BINGLEY. And if the canapés are not arranged in a likeness of my face immediately – you're all for the sack!

CLARA (*indicating a huge tower of cakes behind her*). Is this yin alright here, miss?

MISS BINGLEY *yells at her as they exit – the scene has transformed*.

Scene Eleven (a)

We're at Netherfield Park in party mode. MRS BENNET, LYDIA, ELIZABETH *and* JANE *enter and gawp at the money in evidence around them.*

LYDIA. Fuck me, it's posh!

MRS BENNET. Girls, come here –

> LYDIA *is in the act of licking a cream cake from the side of the tower of cakes, tears herself away. A pre-match huddle forms.*

> (*Handing out hair adornments.*) Now, Jane – your focus is naturally Mr Bingley. We're on the home straight, there. We must *all* compliment him, Miss Bingley – and even the miserable Mr Darcy – on the decor, the entertainment and the finger food. Say it?

ALL. The decor. The entertainment. The finger food.

> TILLIE *enters with a drinks trolley.*

MRS BENNET (*still holding two unaccounted-for fascinators*). Oh! I've left the gift with Mary and Kitty. I'll be back! (*Heading offstage.*) They've invited a lot of soldiers!

> LYDIA *grabs a champagne bottle from* TILLIE*'s trolly and heads off –*

LYDIA. Soldiers?! I've always wanted a go on a pistol! (*Into the wing as exiting – flirtatious.*) Oi! One of you'll give me a lend of your gun, won't you? Oh go on…!

> ELIZABETH *and* JANE *are left looking uncertain.*

TILLIE (*to audience*). I should explain, there's a war on. I know, we've kept that very quiet. But it's true – our men are being called on to fight in France.

> There's this terrible atmosphere… papers scaremongering, saying we're all under threat from foreigners.

> You'll live in more enlightened times I'm sure.

Anyway, groups of redcoats are being stationed all over just now, and one regiment has just arrived here, in Meryton.

MRS BENNET *with her gift bag re-enters.*

ELIZABETH. Anyone seen Charl– ?

MRS BENNET. Uh – ! We are not talking to you, Lizzie, thank you! You are persona non-starter. Now, Jane – seal the deal with this. (*Handing it to her.*)

JANE. What is it?

MRS BENNET. Your secret weapon. Give that to the hosts and we'll be sending out save-the-dates by the end of the week!

JANE *reaches into the bag and pulls out its much smaller contents. It's a mint Viennetta.*

JANE. Vee-ah-neh-ta?

MRS BENNET (*tapping the side of her nose*). Italian.

TILLIE *approaches* MRS BENNET *to serve her from the trolly.* MRS BENNET *holds her glass out.*

(*To* JANE.) Quick – before it melts!

JANE *exits.* ELIZABETH *eats from the tower.*

(*To* TILLIE.) Where's the master, is he hiding from his guests?

TILLIE. I'm not sure. Do the soldiers make you uneasy, madam?

MRS BENNET. Oh no. I feel safer, if anything. And it's nice seeing… men in uniform. For the younger girls, I mean. Obviously *I* wouldn't –

TILLIE. No, madam. After all, you must be in your late / fif–

MRS BENNET. *Thirties*, exactly!

MR WICKHAM *appears somewhere in the audience. Both women have a good look.*

Bloody hell, what's that one called?

TILLIE. Mr George Wickham, I believe.

MRS BENNET (*she growls, openly lustful*). I imagine he keeps his flintlock in a state of… high polish. (*Inhaler.*)

TILLIE (*not up for sex chat*). If you'll excuse me –

ELIZABETH. Mum…! Maybe pace yourself?

MRS BENNET (*exacting revenge – looking offstage*). Oh, look Elizabeth – your cousin. Mr Collins, sir!

MRS BENNET *beckons him over and exits leaving* ELIZABETH *stuck.* COLLINS *enters looking very jolly. Frank Sinatra's 'Love and Marriage' plays low on the stereo.*

COLLINS. All alone, Miss Elizabeth?

ELIZABETH. Actually, I was just going to find –

COLLINS. Good job I arrived to keep you company. I wouldn't want to leave you *all alone for the rest of your life.*

ELIZABETH (*trying to suss him out*). I trust there are no hard feelings between us?

COLLINS (*somehow knowing*). Oh no! Of course not. None at all!

MISS BINGLEY *crosses through the space –* JANE *runs on after her.*

JANE. Miss Bingley! Is Charles with you?

MISS BINGLEY. Oh, Jane. I'm afraid I'm quite busy. Hosting duties, you know.

JANE. Oh, of course. I just wanted to say – it's a wonderful party. Decor. Entertainment. Finger food. (*Holding out the Viennetta.*) This is for you. It's for pudding. Sorry – dessert.

MISS BINGLEY *walks off, ignoring her.* JANE *is left holding the deteriorating Viennetta.*

I'll just give it to one of the servants, then, shall I…? Caroline? Caroline?

JANE *exits after* MISS BINGLEY. DARCY *enters and approaches.*

COLLINS. Ah, Fitzwilliam Darcy! You came to introduce yourself to me?

Beat.

DARCY (*as if this should be obvious*). No.

DARCY *offers an arm.* ELIZABETH *isn't sure which is worse. But she takes it and walks with him.* COLLINS *isn't too bothered – he exits.* ELIZABETH *and* DARCY *are left together. The track changes rather suddenly – Spandau Ballet's 'True'.*

ELIZABETH (*through gritted teeth*). Thank you for that… intervention. I don't suppose you know why he's in such a good mood. Oh, before I forget… (*Non-committal.*) I'd like to compliment you, Bingley and Caroline on the decor, the entertainment and the finger food.

DARCY *doesn't respond.*

I trust you're well?

DARCY *has barely moved a muscle.*

Oh, come on.

DARCY. I'm sorry?

ELIZABETH. I appreciate you saving me from Collins but you must know it's your turn to say something now.

DARCY. My *turn*?

ELIZABETH. It can talk! I asked you how you were. You could either answer, ask me how I am – or open up a new topic altogether.

DARCY. Do you talk as a rule, then, at parties?

ELIZABETH. I think it's encouraged.

DARCY (*boldly*). Listen, now that Collins is out of the way –

ELIZABETH. Yes, I've had enough encounters with Mr Collins for one lifetime.

DARCY. Indeed. But now that he's out of the way, maybe you might like to do some more dancing?

ELIZABETH. What?

DARCY. Maybe, now, you'd care to dance?

ELIZABETH *eyes him suspiciously and misunderstands him completely.*

ELIZABETH. I know that nothing would give you more pleasure than to hear me say 'yes'.

DARCY. That's right –

ELIZABETH. Because all we do in Meryton is dance and sing and drink –

DARCY. No, I –

ELIZABETH. You'd love me to run along and dance so that you can stand in the shadows and scoff at me and my family.

DARCY. I *meant* you and –

ELIZABETH. Well, we do have other interests. Other thoughts. Sometimes I hate to dance. Right now, for example, you couldn't pay me to. Instead I'm going to go and enjoy a proper conversation with one of my friends. So there's your answer.

ELIZABETH *marches off towards* CHARLOTTE. DARCY, *fizzing, leaves.*

Charlotte! I'm having the worst day of my life. First, you know my cousin, Mr Collins? – Oh God, I feel sick even thinking about it – he proposed to me! I felt like saying 'Listen, you conceited, pompous, narrow-minded twat – no sane woman will *ever* marry you.'

CHARLOTTE. I'm going to.

ELIZABETH. Going to what?

CHARLOTTE. Marry him.

ELIZABETH *looks at her. It must be a joke. She chuckles.*

We're engaged.

ELIZABETH. Charlotte, he proposed to *me* this morning.

CHARLOTTE. And you said no. So he proposed to me at lunchtime.

ELIZABETH. Are you serious?

CHARLOTTE *nods*.

But how could – ?

CHARLOTTE. I saw him passing, so I pretended to go out for a walk. So that he'd see me.

ELIZABETH. I meant, how could you agree to this?

CHARLOTTE. I'm not like you. I'm not romantic. I've never gone weak at the knees for *any* man.

ELIZABETH. Then the right man just hasn't come along.

CHARLOTTE. God, you don't know me at all, do you? If you are free to turn Mr Collins down, I am free to accept him.

ELIZABETH. Charlotte, I'm begging –

CHARLOTTE. Stop talking, Liz. When you're ready to congratulate me on this, maybe we'll have something to say to each other.

ELIZABETH. Charlotte – !

CHARLOTTE *exits*. ELIZABETH *whirrs around distressed – a man is holding out a drink for her. It's* GEORGE WICKHAM *in his dashing red coat.*

WICKHAM. Rough night?

ELIZABETH. No thank you, I think I've had enough.

WICKHAM. Oh, you misunderstand me, no strings. I just saw a beautiful lady who deserved to be having a much better time and I wanted to… give her this – (*Handing it over.*) and leave her in peace.

He goes as if to exit back into the audience then positively counts the seconds until –

ELIZABETH. No, it's okay. Stay. Sorry – rude of me.

WICKHAM. Perhaps you could use some air? (*Offering cigarettes*.)

They move off and SERVANTS *form the scene*.

Scene Eleven (b)

Lights shift – we're at the trademen's entrance. One large recycling bin. One SERVANT *idly strums an acoustic guitar alongside. The stars shine. It's all strangely romantic*.

WICKHAM. So – what's the story tonight, miss…?

ELIZABETH. Elizabeth. Bennet. (*To the cigarette packet*.) No thanks. (*To the question*.) I think I might have turned my mother and my best friend against me forever.

WICKHAM. Not possible. Who could stay angry at you?

All at once, WICKHAM *turns – he looks incredibly handsome. At this moment, the bin lid had started to open and another* MUSICIAN *appears from inside, adding to the romantic underscore. Hypnotised,* ELIZABETH *takes the cigarette*.

ELIZABETH. I never meant to hurt anyone. I was just… following my heart.

WICKHAM. Well then you are entirely in the right. (*Intensely – holding her gaze*.) There's nothing in the world more important than that.

ELIZABETH (*captivated*). What did you say your name was?

WICKHAM. George Wickham. (*A third* SERVANT *popping up to light his cigarette*.) How do you know the hosts?

ELIZABETH. Neighbours. Friends, I suppose. Well – of the Bingleys. Darcy's just… visiting, I think.

WICKHAM (*sizing her up*). Is Darcy… someone you'd call a friend, too?

ELIZABETH. I…

Beat

I can't stand him.

WICKHAM. He's always disliked me. One of the boys
overheard him say if he catches me here, he'll have me
thrown out.

ELIZABETH. Why?

WICKHAM (*faux-conflicted*). Ah, I'd rather not say.

ELIZABETH. Did something happen between you two?

WICKHAM. It was years ago and… I wouldn't want anyone in
Meryton to think less of him. Alright, just between us.

WICKHAM*'s moment. He begins his performance.
Melodrama. The romantic* MUSICIANS *underscore this with
something dramatic. The recycling* SERVANT *produces a
pair of maracas as if from thin air at the perfect moment.*

Darcy's father was my godfather. A wonderful, kind man. On
his deathbed, he promised to leave me a sum of money so
that I could train in a good profession. I wasn't always going
to be a humble soldier, Elizabeth. No – I was meant for the
church.

ELIZABETH. What happened?

WICKHAM. Darcy spread vicious, unfounded rumours about
me being extravagant with money. He contested the will, the
judge ruled in his favour – and Darcy kept the money for
himself.

ELIZABETH. No?!

WICKHAM. Yes! My dear godfather's wishes remain
unfulfilled, I have been left near penniless, having to abandon
my dreams of a good living in the clergy and forced into the
military where every day I lay my life on the line.

All because of Darcy's spite!

Slam! A SERVANT *closes the bin. Music out.* ELIZABETH
is stunned.

ELIZABETH. The bastard! Do people know?

WICKHAM. I doubt it. But I won't be the one to tell them.
I loved my godfather too much. And anyway, Darcy's...
deceptive. He's good at turning on the charm. People believe
him. You see how ladies flock to him!

ELIZABETH. For his money, maybe. But who could ever love
him?

WICKHAM. Hardly matters. He'll marry Miss de Bourgh.

ELIZABETH. Who?

WICKHAM. His cousin. Lady Catherine's daughter.

ELIZABETH. Lady fucking Catherine...

WICKHAM. Lady fucking Catherine of Rosings, yes. She's
Darcy's aunt. She intends to marry Darcy off to her daughter
– and what Lady Catherine wants, she gets.

ELIZABETH *is amazed*.

ELIZABETH. So he's as good as engaged? Caroline Bingley
has been wasting her time, then!... She's always flirting and
showing off that she's pals with... thingy – Darcy's little
sister. You'll know – ! What's the wee sister called...?

WICKHAM *turns pale*.

– Georgiana!

WICKHAM *spits out his drink*.

(*Not noticing*.) That's it. Georgiana Darcy! You must have
met her, when you knew the family?

WICKHAM (*panicking*). Maybe. No. Barely. I'm sorry – I
thought I could talk about the past but – (*Laying it on thick*.)
My God, the feelings are still just so raw...!

ELIZABETH. Oh, of course. I'm so sorry. How insensitive of me.

She touches his hand, tenderly. Beat. They look at each other.

Look at the state of us two, eh?

WICKHAM. Quite the pair.

They gaze at each other – then lean in for a kiss, but an amplified voice booms from the house –

MRS BENNET (*unseen but amplified*). **How do you switch it on?**

ELIZABETH. No, Mum...

WICKHAM. What on earth – ?

Lights up on MRS BENNET.

MRS BENNET. **Oh it is on!**

Scene Eleven (c)

We're back indoors at the party. MRS BENNET on a plinth – she has had a lot to drink. She holds a microphone and everyone stops to listen to her. ELIZABETH stands horrified but WICKHAM skulks off lest he draw attention to himself.

MRS BENNET. **Good evening, good evening... good evening.**

ELIZABETH. Mum!

MRS BENNET. **Don't worry, Lizzie, I'm not going to sing – I just wanted to raise a toast to finding The One! Now, I'm not saying I'd know these days, my husband hasn't touched me in twelve years – but the host of this party has found love and will very soon be engaged to a beautiful mystery girl from our own village!**

ELIZABETH. Please get down.

JANE. No, Mum... (*Head in her hands.*)

MRS BENNET. **Shush, it's okay, Jane, I didn't say your name. So let's raise our glasses – to proposals! To permanent financial security! To true love!**

JANE whirrs around crying – huge black mascara tears down her face.

JANE. Waaaaa!

MRS BENNET. Jane?

MARY. She's drunk!

JANE (*to* MARY). One of the soldiers kept topping me up.

ELIZABETH. Never mind that, why are you crying? Darling –
    what's wrong, tell us?

JANE. It's Bingley.

ELIZABETH. What's he said? I'll kill him.

JANE. That's just it. He said nothing…

    But now, out of nowhere –

    He's leaving.

    Moving back to London.

    Tomorrow.

MRS BENNET. London?!

JANE. I'm never going to see him again!

    She can't speak for crying. ELIZABETH *hugs her.*

MRS BENNET. Bingley's dumped you?!

    JANE *bawls.*

    This is all your fault, Elizabeth! Your sharp tongue and
    muddy stockings probably put him off!

ELIZABETH. I thought you weren't talking to me.

MRS BENNET. You will *definitely* marry Collins now – I don't
    care what you think of him!

ELIZABETH. Too late. He's engaged to Charlotte.

    Beat.

MRS BENNET. *What?!*

ELIZABETH. He's engaged to Charlotte. They're getting
    married.

MRS BENNET. Charlotte Lucas will inherit our home? Well, we're done for! I don't believe it – this morning I had two daughters ready to marry –

JANE *bawls*.

Now I have bugger all! You are a selfish girl, Elizabeth Bennet! Why were you so stupid?!

ELIZABETH. Listen to yourself! Your problem is that –

MRS BENNET. *My* problem is ungrateful children!

ELIZABETH. Are we supposed to be grateful for having to manage your neuroses?

MRS. BENNET *slaps her in the face*.

MRS BENNET. Stop trying to be clever! Look where that has got you.

Beat of shock. All stare in silence at this.

Then –

The intro from Rigoletto's 'La Donna è Mobile' plays loud. The girls turn to see where it's coming from. MARY *is on the stairs and has found a mic.*

ELIZABETH. No, Mary! Don't do it!

MRS BENNET. Someone stop that girl singing!

ELIZABETH *runs upstairs to wrestle* MARY *for the mic.*

Stop her!

ELIZABETH. / Come on, Mary, let the other girls have a chance…

MARY. Let me have my moment! / You never even let me try!

MRS BENNET. It's for your own good!

JANE *looks panicked – she is convulsing.*

Jane – ? Jane, what's wrong with you?!

All stop and look at JANE *who does the only thing she can and violently throws up into the rare Japanese vase.* MISS BINGLEY *runs on screaming – horrified.*

MISS BINGLEY (*running at* JANE). My vase! Give me that! Give it to me!

JANE *runs away and tries to keep hold of it with a misguided notion of saving the situation.*

Oh you're disgusting! (*Grabbing* JANE *by the hair.*)

ELIZABETH *spots this and abandons* MARY *who continues up the stairs to the next floor.*

ELIZABETH. Don't you lay a finger on my sister, ya stuck-up shite! (*Running down the stairs again to get involved.*)

JANE. Lizzie, no…

LIZZIE *grabs* MISS BINGLEY *but this sets off a chain reaction that causes* JANE *to drop the vase which smashes. Music intensifies.*

LYDIA *runs on.*

LYDIA. Paaaaaaaartaaaaaaay!

LYDIA *is holding a huge flintlock pistol. Everyone ducks, petrified.*

MISS BINGLEY. Where on earth did you get that?

LYDIA. One of those nice soldiers gave it to me, I don't know how it works, though –

BANG! LYDIA *fires the pistol into the air. The bullet hits the chandelier which has been hoisted up high since the top of the show. Everyone scatters, screaming. The great object stops just shy of the enormous tower of cakes – but* MRS BENNET *flies into these regardless in the panic, sending them everywhere. The room is a bombsight.*

MISS BINGLEY (*leaping for the gun*). I'll kill you all – !

A bell in the proscenium arch rings.

The SERVANTS *all look up, startled. They drop character.*

CLARA (*totally sober*). I completely forgot we were still at work. (*Throwing off her dress.*)

ANNE. Me too. (*Lowering the plinth – to* TILLIE.) Sorry.

TILLIE. No problem. What a mess we've made…

CLARA. We got totally carried away there.

Another bell rings. Increased pressure. Others take their costumes off.

FLO. And we lost track of time. The masters will be wanting their gin and tonic. (*Looking at audience.*) Oh you should probably have a drink, too.

ANNE. It's going to take ten minutes to clear all this up…

TILLIE. Ten? No – twenty minutes!

Ringing bells – all rush off.

You go! See you when we've taken care of all this!

Interval

Perhaps during the interval the occasional SERVANT *is seen behind the theatre bar, or serving a drink to someone sat in the auditorium. They may walk along the queue to the ladies' with a plunger complaining that someone's blocked a toilet again…*

ACT TWO

Scene One

As the act begins, a single spotlight on TILLIE *in a dynamic pose at the piano. She sings Bonnie Tyler's 'Holding Out for a Hero' beginning slowly and dramatically. Then the pace increases and the husbandless* BENNET SISTERS *join in, singing of their plight.*

In lieu of the final line, MRS BENNET *demands 'I need a top-up!'*

All music and lights out at once as TILLIE *is placed firmly back in reality.*

MRS BENNET. Tillie!

TILLIE *looks blank.*

TILLIE. What?

MRS BENNET. I need a top-up!

TILLIE. Pardon, madam.

MRS BENNET. You were in a world of your own there…

TILLIE *pours* MRS BENNET *a Baileys. The space can now be seen clearly. Longbourn. Christmas decorations hanging limply. Paper hats from crackers worn forlornly.* JANE *and* ELIZABETH *with* MRS BENNET *as she cries theatrically and drinks immoderately. The end of 'Holding Out for a Hero' now plays reedily from a stereo. It transitions into Christmas music.*

Imagine, Jane – going into the new year as 'Mrs Bingley'. And your children would have been so good-looking…

JANE *looks hurt.*

ELIZABETH. Let's change the subject.

MRS BENNET. All this has really taken its toll on my health... (*Swig*.) To think, a man that nice, flirting with you, *misleading* us –

JANE. I'm sure Bingley didn't set out to mislead anyone.

MRS BENNET. – and just buggering off to London. What was wrong with Netherfield Park? He said he liked it.

JANE. He's allowed to move around. Young men do as they please.

ELIZABETH. *Bingley* won't have had any say in the matter.

JANE. Liz, what's the point – ?

MRS BENNET. What kind of Christmas can a person have in *London*, anyway? And knowing that we are to be left for dead! The baby Jesus will be spinning in his grave!

ELIZABETH (*ignoring* JANE). Bingley's not to blame, Mum. His sister was trying to drag him back to London from the moment she laid eyes on us. And I bet Darcy colluded with her.

MRS BENNET. People are cunning!

ELIZABETH. The more I learn about Darcy, the more I'd believe him capable of anything.

MRS BENNET. I know! Fancy denying sexy Mr – I mean poor Mr Wickham his inheritance. Someone should expose that Darcy.

JANE. Stop! There doesn't always have to be a guilty party. Has it not occurred to you that maybe I just wasn't good enough for Bingley?

ELIZABETH. Jane, he was in love with you.

JANE. Please! Don't use that word. Not if you can't be sure.

Beat. She calms herself.

Look – these are not evil people. Caroline still writes me letters, now and then.

ELIZABETH. Yes, saying – (*Mocking tone.*) 'how much nicer' London is, how 'we'll probably never leave', and how 'Bingley's getting on so well with Darcy's little sister Georgiana – ooh what a lovely pair *they* would make'. It's obvious! She's just trying to cut you out, Jane.

MRS GARDINER *enters with* TILLIE.

TILLIE. Beg your pardon, madam. Mrs Gardiner is leaving now.

MRS GARDINER. Well, it has been a *lovely* Christm–

MRS BENNET (*collapsing in her arms*). Don't leave us…!

TILLIE (*turning to the audience*). Sorry. Rude of me. Please meet Mrs Gardiner.

Or as the Bennet girls call her, 'Aunty G'. An absolute diamond. She visits every Christmas for an update on the girls' love lives. No shortage of gossip this year – what with the scandal of Wickham's stolen inheritance. Turns out, Mrs Gardiner knew the Darcy family very well when Fitzwilliam Darcy was just a wee boy.

MRS GARDINER. Thank you for having m–

MRS BENNET. Pray for the girls, won't you? At least Mr Wickham seems fond of our Elizabeth. Not that we'd last long on one soldier's wage. I wonder if he has any other assets…? (*Turning all attention to her drink.*)

ELIZABETH. Ah, the spirit of Christmas.

MRS GARDINER *between the two eldest daughters.*

MRS GARDINER. Now, I'm sure you know better than to choose someone charming and handsome, Liz!

ELIZABETH. I'd settle for someone half as handsome as George Wickham.

MRS GARDINER. So, you *are* fond of him?

ELIZABETH (*coy*). Maybe.

MRS GARDINER (*pulling* ELIZABETH *close for a private word*). I don't remember all the details of that trouble around Wickham's inheritance but just – be cautious, won't you?

ELIZABETH (*laughing*). Don't worry. If I was the type to rush into marriage, I'd be Mrs Collins by now! What a miserable existence that would –

ELIZABETH *is suddenly consumed by sadness. She realises whose life she's describing.*

Oh poor Charlotte.

Beat.

Then – fast – girls pulling at MRS GARDINER *each time she makes a move to leave.*

MRS GARDINER. Well, I should probably get going –

JANE. I'll probably be okay, Aunty G.

MRS GARDINER. It's tough when you have a… 'romantic disappointment'. But you definitely will.

Right, I'll –

ELIZABETH. Do you think Charlotte and I could still be friends?

MRS GARDINER. It's never too late to make amends. Make a visit, even.

Okay –

JANE. I mean, sure. It might have been exciting –

ELIZABETH. A visit? To their home? Oh, but Collins…!

MRS GARDINER. If you want her back, it would be time well spent.

So –

JANE. And, okay, yes, he may have made me happier than anyone or anything ever has –

ELIZABETH. You're right. I should go to Kent –

JANE. But he was only one man. One perfect man. (*Tearing up*.) And why would anyone care about losing that?

Bang! MRS BENNET, *whose head had been lolling, collapses drunk face-first into a tin of Quality Street.* MRS GARDINER *pulls her up to prevent suffocation.*

MRS GARDINER (*spinning plates*). Perhaps you'd like to come with me, Jane? Take a little break from –

A pronounced snore from MRS BENNET.

Everything?

JANE. London? I don't know. Isn't there a chance I might run into – ?

MRS GARDINER (*knowing*). Oh, I doubt it. It's a huge city.

JANE. I'm not sure I –

MRS BENNET *wakes herself with a snore, takes in the forlorn scene and bursts into tears once more.*

JANE/ELIZABETH. Tillie, can you pack me a bag?

TILLIE *nods, smiling and moves off. The scene transforms.* JANE *and* ELIZABETH *stand downstage and share a goodbye embrace.* JANE *finds a way to share a little humour.*

JANE. Have fun with Mr Collins.

ELIZABETH *giggles.* JANE *moves off. We see* ELIZABETH's *face change as the reality sets in.*

ELIZABETH. You better write to me every day! I'm going to need something to keep me going…

Scene Two

Lights up on JANE *in her aunty's modest London home, looking a little vulnerable and lonely.* (*Letters in* **bold**.)

JANE. **Dearest Elizabeth, I've been in London for...** (*Stops to count.*) **twenty-three minutes now. I think it's time I wrote to Caroline Bingley. She'll be thrilled to hear I'm in town.**

Lights up on ELIZABETH *in* COLLINS' *beige-as-hell home.* COLLINS *and* CHARLOTTE *exhibit their house.* ELIZABETH *trying to avoid her hosts.*

ELIZABETH. **Dearest Jane –**

COLLINS. Now – you'll be keen to see the curtains! (*Exits to another room.*)

ELIZABETH. **Kill me now. I've arrived in Kent. But where's my old pal Charlotte gone? They do say that marriage changes you... Collins seems to be the exception. He's more 'himself' than ever.**

JANE. **Dear Liz, it's my second week in London and still no word from Caroline. I only sent her four letters so maybe – one more? It will simply be that they were lost in the post. She wouldn't ever ignore me on purpose.**

Would she?

ELIZABETH. **Jane, I'd love to be the one to offer you hope in mankind but I've only been here a fortnight and today I had to hide in a linen cupboard for some 'alone time'.**

COLLINS (*re-entering*). I'm sure you agree that the best feature of the garden is the view of Lady Catherine de Bourgh's own house – (*Reverently.*) Rosings! Do you see it, Elizabeth? Are you looking? I don't think you're looking.

ELIZABETH. **And Darcy's aunt, Lady Catherine... Lives right next door at Rosings! With her daughter 'Miss de Bourgh'. You know, the one intended for Darcy to marry.** (*Gossipy.*) **I've seen her going past in her carriage – she's** white as a ghost, always sneezing and utterly miserable. (*Beat.*) A perfect wife for him, really.

JANE. Dear Liz, I couldn't wait any longer. I went round to Caroline Bingley's house. She looked very surprised to see me. I told her about all the letters I'd been sending. She agreed! They must have all been lost in the post. I had to leave straight away because she was too busy to see me, but she promised to visit me at Aunty G's soon. Oh – did you hear about Mr Wickham?

ELIZABETH. Mary wrote me that Wickham's got a fancy woman –?

JANE. And no one knows who it is!

ELIZABETH. It's weird. I don't feel anything. If I loved him – I'd hate the girl's guts, wouldn't I?

JANE (*hope fading*). Dear Liz. A full month and still no visit from Caroline. Realised she might be calling whenever I'm out so, now, I just stay at home. By the door.

COLLINS (*re-entering*). Miss Elizabeth?

JANE. There's probably some perfectly logical –

COLLINS. Coo-ee! Excellent news!

JANE. Oh Liz. (*Pained.*) Maybe you were right.

ELIZABETH. What is it?

JANE (*crestfallen*). I should have listened. People really *are* cruel and selfish.

COLLINS. Now you've been here a full month, Lady Catherine has decided to invite you to dinner.

JANE. The Bingley's want nothing to do with me. How could I have been so stupid?

COLLINS. But the event is tonight, so we'll need to spend the rest of the day preparing you.

ELIZABETH. *Preparing* me – ?

COLLINS. Otherwise, when the time comes, the grandeur of Rosings may cause you to pass out, right there on the exquisite marble flooring.

JANE. **I give up. I'm just going to… go home.**

ELIZABETH (*rushed*). **I'm so sorry, beautiful girl. But you are better off without them. I'll write to you at Mum and Dad's soon.**

JANE. **Yours, et cetera –**

ELIZABETH. **Elizabeth.**

JANE. **Jane.**

Beat.

ELIZABETH/JANE. **Kiss.**

COLLINS. Come along!

COLLINS, ELIZABETH *and* CHARLOTTE *move downstage centre.*

Scene Three

Sound and lights in! – The impressive Rosings.

COLLINS (*to* ELIZABETH). I wouldn't worry about your dress.

ELIZABETH. I'm sorry?

COLLINS. That dress. Don't worry. Lady Catherine won't necessarily think any less of you.

FLO (*to the audience*). Welcome to Rosings.

FLO *sees the guests.*

I will let Lady Catherine know that you are all here, sir. (*Running up the stairs.*)

COLLINS. You must. And be quick about it! (*To* ELIZABETH.)
Do we need to recap the differences between the various
types of spoon you may be dealing with this evening?

FLO (*from the high stairs*). Mr and Mrs Collins, Miss Bennet –
I present, Lady Catherine de Bourgh!

A ridiculously pompous entrance – lights, music and fanfare.
LADY CATHERINE *is wearing an impractically huge and
imposing costume adorned with red roses.* CHARLOTTE
curtsies, COLLINS *applauds and bows, and* ELIZABETH
stares – eventually taking the hint to also curtsy.

Will I tell cook that you are almost ready to eat, Your
Ladyship?

LADY CATHERINE. Of course not! How could we possibly
begin before my nephew has arrived?

FLO *scurries off.*

ELIZABETH. Your nephew is coming?

LADY CATHERINE. Oh. Are you speaking to me? You do that
very directly, don't you?

ELIZABETH. I appreciate I've not introduced myself yet –

LADY CATHERINE. I know who you are, Miss Elizabeth
Bennet. I am trusting that as one of the Collins'
acquaintances you will be a mannered, sensible sort of
person?

Beat.

Well?!

ELIZABETH. Oh – was that a question?

LADY CATHERINE. Whether it was or not, what on earth
could you mean by offering another question in response?

CHARLOTTE (*saving it*). Lady Catherine – I know Elizabeth's
delighted to have received your invitation. She is always a
charming dinner guest.

LADY CATHERINE (*placated*). Yes. Well, I will be the judge of that. (*Examining* ELIZABETH.) What kind of carriage does your father keep, Miss Bennet?

As ELIZABETH *goes to speak,* DARCY *runs in.*

DARCY. I must apologise sincerely for... (*Seeing* ELIZABETH.) being late.

They lock eyes.

LADY CATHERINE. This is my nephew, Miss Bennet.

ELIZABETH. Yes...

LADY CATHERINE. Visiting from Derbyshire. He is not ordinarily late.

ELIZABETH (*to* DARCY). No. In fact, his timing is often astounding.

LADY CATHERINE (*straining her ears*). What are you saying?

ELIZABETH. I was just agreeing with you, Lady Catherine.

LADY CATHERINE. Well, if you have something to say, say it aloud to the whole room. I must have my share in the conversation if the topic is time-keeping. Punctuality is a sign of good breeding and proper manners. Luckily, my nephew is beholden of both – but those of a lower rank cannot *ever* afford to be late. Are you a punctual person, Miss Bennet? How large is your house? How many of you live in it? Siblings? Any married?

ELIZABETH (*efficiently – counting on her fingers*). Try to be. Big enough. All of us. Five girls. Not a one married.

LADY CATHERINE. Do you draw?

ELIZABETH. No.

LADY CATHERINE. What – *none* of you? Why ever not? Do you even net purses? Cover screens? Paint tables? Sing?

ELIZABETH. I can sing a little.

LADY CATHERINE. Ah, then we'll hear you.

A couple of beats.

ELIZABETH. Oh, you mean – ?

LADY CATHERINE. Now. Yes. Naturally. (*Indicating the piano*.) Accompany her, won't you, Mrs Collins? There is a suitable piece there, ready.

CHARLOTTE *hands* ELIZABETH *the sheet music and a mic, then begins to play the opening bars*.

ELIZABETH (*to* CHARLOTTE). What is this song?

LADY CATHERINE. I thought you were a singer! It is the single most celebrated composition by the greatest musician in the country: my other nephew, Mr Christopher de Bourgh.

ELIZABETH *sings the first verse of Chris de Burgh's 'The Lady in Red'*.

COLLINS (*to* LADY CATHERINE). Doubtless inspired by your beauty.

LADY CATHERINE (*firmly*). Shhh!

ELIZABETH *sings the second verse and chorus*. LADY CATHERINE *and* COLLINS *listen, while* DARCY *is drawn slowly to the singer of the song*.

ELIZABETH *begins to meet* DARCY*'s gaze as she continues to sing*.

The piano continues under the dialogue. COLLINS *and* LADY CATHERINE *in a De Bourghian reverie*.

ELIZABETH. I see you've come to try and put me off, Darcy. But you should know, the more you intimidate me, the more courage I have. I'm like that.

DARCY. But you also amuse yourself by saying things you don't really mean.

ELIZABETH. You have the measure of me! I *beg* you not to reveal my true character, here in this... elite company.

DARCY *smirks. Beat*.

Of course, there are one or two things I could expose about *your* true character.

DARCY. I have no idea what you're referring to, Miss Bennet –
but, I assure you, I'm not afraid of you.

ELIZABETH. Oh really?

A challenge –

Beat.

– Accepted!

(*Announcing it to the room.*) This man!

CHARLOTTE *stops playing. Everyone stares.*

Denied a *poor soul* their rightful...

ELIZABETH *feels the eyes on her, weighs up her choices.*
And makes one.

Rightful singing partner. Me. He denied me a singing partner.
When we first met. At the town ball. 'Cause, you know – it
was a duet.

LADY CATHERINE. Perhaps he was deterring you from
singing in public, Miss Bennet. Gracious intervention.
Something for which he can always be relied upon. Why,
only last month you saved that misguided friend of yours
from disaster, Darcy.

DARCY (*panicked*). I wouldn't say that –

LADY CATHERINE. He would have thrown away his future
on that common country girl if you hadn't persuaded him to
move back to London.

ELIZABETH. Sorry?

DARCY. Now –

ELIZABETH. Exactly which friend was this, Lady Catherine?

LADY CATHERINE. I don't recall the man's name. But Darcy
knows a bad match as well as he knows a good one.

ELIZABETH. Does he...?

LADY CATHERINE (*oblivious*). Speaking of which, I apologise that my daughter cannot sit next to you this evening, Darcy. She's still ill, in bed – but sends her affectionate regards.

COLLINS. What a pity! Miss de Bourgh is so fond of you, Darcy.

ELIZABETH (*sarcastically*). Of course she is. I'd love to know more about your heroics, Darcy – this common country girl you 'saved' your friend from?

CHARLOTTE (*attempting to save the evening*). Liz!

Everyone waits for CHARLOTTE *to speak.*

(*Clutching at straws.*) Your mother! – Is she well?

ELIZABETH. Not in her opinion. She's a hypochondriac.

CHARLOTTE (*desperately*). Your sisters, then!

ELIZABETH. *Jane's* had a tough time. (*Turning back to* DARCY.) I don't suppose you bumped into her recently, Darcy?

DARCY. What?

ELIZABETH. Jane. My sister. She's been in London for a month now. You're often there visiting Bingley and Caroline. Perhaps *they've* seen her?

DARCY (*avoiding her gaze*). I wouldn't know.

ELIZABETH. No. No of course not. It's a big place. So easy for two people to just… miss each other entirely. Especially if… I don't know, say, letters get lost or –

DARCY. I'll – !

Seeing the polite company around him.

…I'll tell them to hurry up with dinner.

He exits. The space transforms.

Scene Four

The Parsonage. The clock sounds for the top of the hour.

COLLINS. Miss Elizabeth! Time for my morning recitation! Will it be Tredwell's *Preliminary Discourse on the Study of Modern Botany* or Lord Chambers' *Compendium of Basic Geological Principles*? Eenie, meanie, m–

ELIZABETH (*calling the* SERVANT). Clara – can you recommend any more walks?

CLARA. You've already covered Master Collins' grounds, miss. There may be other routes, but they'd be quite ambitious.

ELIZABETH. I don't mind if it's a really, really long walk.

CLARA. Well, racking my brains – you could...

The scene transforms – the outdoors. ELIZABETH *makes her way over the terrain.*

(*Purposeful.*) March to the gate at the end of the field and turn left!

ELIZABETH. Right!

CLARA. Look for the stream just beyond Badger's Mount and use the stepping stones to cross.

ELIZABETH. Aha!

CLARA. After fifty yards, you'll reach a stile to an open field, vault it, cross the field diagonally –

ELIZABETH. Woah there!

CLARA. Watch out for the sheep –

ANNE. Baa!

CLARA. It's lambing season. And in minutes you'll reach beautiful Meenfield Wood. You'll probably notice the extraordinary bird life here –

But make sure to head up the incline to see a spectacular view of the surrounds and town below.

ELIZABETH *takes in the view* – CLARA *plays the harp*.

ELIZABETH (*her breath taken away by it*). Oh, what are men to rocks and mountains!

CLARA. Turn right at the view point and after a hundred yards you'll reach the best part of all. The most picturesque little bramble-filled valley where sunlight streams through tall pine trees and –

DARCY *is in the valley.*

DARCY. Miss Elizabeth.

All music out.

ELIZABETH (*panting, pissed off*). Oh… It's you.

DARCY. You're running around in the woods.

ELIZABETH. I am.

Beat.

DARCY. Why?

ELIZABETH. I like it. Why else?

Beat.

DARCY. Do you walk often?

ELIZABETH. A bit.

Beat.

DARCY. It's stunning. Do you not think?

ELIZABETH. Yup. Shame not to walk it every day.

DARCY. At around this time, every day?

ELIZABETH (*suspicious of him*). No. I'll vary it. Then you can enjoy your walks uninterrupted. Good day, Mr Darcy.

She walks away. DARCY *flounders.*

DARCY. Well, I'm going a little farther down the valley if – ?

ELIZABETH. I'm going a different way so – (*Catching her thumb.*) Ah, bloody brambles!

DARCY. Please! One moment!

She stops.

ELIZABETH (*angry*). What?

He looks at her – transfixed. Beat.

You've stopped talking again, Mr Darcy.

DARCY (*remembering himself*). Sorry. I'll let you – Just –

Careful. Brambles.

They part. DARCY *cringes and then moves purposefully off. The space transforms.*

Scene Five

ELIZABETH *is back at the Parsonage.* CHARLOTTE *sits with her embroidery.*

ELIZABETH. Wasn't Darcy supposed to leave yesterday? Because I saw him in the woods just before I hurt my –

CHARLOTTE. He's extended his stay.

ELIZABETH. Again?

CHARLOTTE. Needed a couple more days, he said.

ELIZABETH. You really prefer this room? Isn't it quite dark? And small? The front parlour is *enormous*, airy, light!

CHARLOTTE. Mr Collins certainly prefers that room. He can usually be found in there.

ELIZABETH. Oh. And you want to sit in *this* room? ...Alone?

CHARLOTTE. I'm not alone, I'm with you. I see Mr Collins every day. Distance is healthy for us. You, I haven't seen in a very long time so... I would like to be in the same room as you.

ELIZABETH. I think even if you saw me every day – even if it was you and me living here together! – we'd be enjoying the view in that nice big front parlour every day instead. (*Her thumb throbs, and she looks down at it.*)

CHARLOTTE. Yes I think… if it were you and I living here together…

ELIZABETH. Imagine!

CHARLOTTE. …Imagine. But if it were you and I… (*Heart racing.*) the truth is, I think whichever room you preferred… I'd like to sit in it with you.

ELIZABETH *is looking down.* CHARLOTTE *cannot tell if she's contemplating what she just said.*

Liz –

ELIZABETH (*totally distracted, nursing her bramble-barbed thumb*). Hmm? What's that – ?

CHARLOTTE *knows it is over.*

CHARLOTTE. Nothing.

ELIZABETH (*oblivious*). Sorry, I cut my thumb really badly on the brambles.

Beat.

What was so wrong with my Jane?

CHARLOTTE. Put it out of your mind, Liz.

ELIZABETH. But I can't stop hearing Darcy congratulating himself on 'saving' his friend from a terrible marriage.

CHARLOTTE. It could have been a different friend.

ELIZABETH. But could it *really*? Does the miserable bastard have other friends?

CHARLOTTE. Please, Elizabeth, Mr Collins dislikes bad language.

ELIZABETH (*amused*). Fuck off? (*Realising* CHARLOTTE*'s serious.*) Oh. Sorry. It's just – who wouldn't like Jane? She's all loveliness! But still – Darcy wants Bingley to marry his little sister Georgiana, then he can shack up with weedy Miss de Bourgh and that'll be quite the neat arrangement for everyone's bank balances! – What do you think?

ELIZABETH looks at CHARLOTTE. CHARLOTTE *looks at her embroidery.*

CHARLOTTE. Don't let it upset you.

ELIZABETH. But sometimes it's okay to get upset. Things can even feel better afterwards. Charlotte – ?

CLARA enters – she is surprised at the tension in the room and regrets her entrance.

CLARA (*to* CHARLOTTE). Beg your pardon, madam – but Master Collins has asked for you. He wants a second opinion...

CHARLOTTE. On?

CLARA hesitates.

(*Impatient.*) *On?*

CLARA (*embarrassed*). On whether... it's infected.

CHARLOTTE *stands. She seems to brace herself. She leaves.* CLARA *hands* ELIZABETH *her letter-writing microphone.*

ELIZABETH. **Dear Jane –**

DARCY enters.

DARCY. Miss Elizabeth.

She jumps.

He's almost shaking.

I'm so sorry. Did I startle you?

ELIZABETH (*coldly*). No. I was just writing to my sister. They're in the front parlour.

DARCY. No. I'm – (*Faltering for a moment*.) One of Lady Catherine's servants mentioned that your thumb was still sore.

ELIZABETH. No.

DARCY. Oh. Only I wondered, if I could get you anything? Something to soothe it?

ELIZABETH. I'm fine.

DARCY. It's…

Beat. DARCY *takes a deep breath*.

It's no use.

This feeling just won't go away.

I've tried to supress it. But I've failed.

I have to tell you, Elizabeth, how strongly I admire and love you.

ELIZABETH *looks up at him for the first time. She is stunned to silence*.

(*Everything now tumbling out*.) And I could never have imagined! You! – the inconvenience of it all – but there's nothing to be done. I have fallen. And it is a love strong enough to have overcome all my better judgement, all my efforts to deny it, all the inferiority of your connections. And so I have a question for you – (*Reaching for the mic*.) I'm sure you'll know how hard this is for me…

The SERVANTS *begin the accompaniment and* DARCY *starts to sing, utterly wooden. David Cassidy's 'I Think I Love You'*.

At the words 'Let me ask you to your face – ' he leaps to one knee. The rock is enormous.

Elizabeth Bennet – will you marry me?

A couple of beats. He looks at her.

It's your turn to say something now, Miss Elizabeth. You'll
appreciate the anxiety a man feels building up to this
moment. But for the sake of our future happiness – I was
willing to go through with it.

Beat.

ELIZABETH. I think I'm supposed to say thank you and tell
you how flattered and overwhelmed I am. Tear up a bit… all
that.

DARCY. Okay?

ELIZABETH. But I can't. I don't thank you. I'm not flattered.
So, no. I won't marry you.

The SERVANTS *shuffle off awkwardly.*

DARCY. Is that it?

ELIZABETH. Yep. And, by the way, I'm not one of those ladies
who refuses in order to accept later. So don't ask a second
time.

DARCY. I wouldn't! Maybe if I were lucky I'd hear *why* you're
rejecting me in this *heartless* way, but I suppose that doesn't
matter, does it? The answer is no.

ELIZABETH. Well, maybe if I was lucky, I'd hear why you
decided to combine a proposal with a selection of insults!
Saying you loved me despite your 'better judgement'? That
would be reason enough to say no – but we both know that
there's more to it than that!

DARCY. I don't know what you –

ELIZABETH. Even if you had asked nicely, do you honestly
think that I could marry the man who intentionally and
maybe even permanently broke my sister's heart? Bingley
didn't want to go back to London. He loved my sister. I don't
recognise her, Darcy. She was perfect goodness. Now she's
broken. And you had a hand in it.

DARCY. Not just a hand – I did everything in my power to
separate them.

ELIZABETH. ...such a bastard!

DARCY. I was concerned for Bingley. I've obviously showed a lot more care for his happiness in marriage than I have for my own –

ELIZABETH. I know about you stealing Wickham's inheritance, too. Was that out of innocent 'concern', as well? Ruining a man's life for your own financial gain?

DARCY. So *that* is what you think of me?! *That's* the kind of man you think I am? If that were true I really would be despicable!

ELIZABETH. You are!

DARCY. Elizabeth – I could have broken a hundred hearts, stolen a thousand inheritances – it wouldn't have mattered, so long as I'd flattered your ego.

ELIZABETH. What?

DARCY. If I had told you that I liked your boring little home town, your insufferable family – and that 'from the moment I laid eyes on you I knew I loved you' – you'd probably be my fiancée by now.

ELIZABETH. You're deluded.

DARCY. Because you are proud. But I'm not ashamed of how I asked because I was telling the truth. I did hesitate. You are not perfect. It was difficult.

ELIZABETH (*lowing her voice, anger simmering*). Well, it was easy for me. You would never have received any other response. Because from the first moment *I* laid eyes on *you*... I could see what an arrogant, selfish, *dull* man you were. Listen carefully when I say, you are the last person on the planet who I would ever, ever marry.

Beat.

DARCY *feels his heart quietly break.*

DARCY. That's enough, I think.

You're right, I probably don't know you at all.

He leaves.

After being stoic throughout this – on his exit, something changes in ELIZABETH. *She is overwhelmed by a combination of anger, shock and upset. Sleep seems unlikely.*

The SERVANTS *enter with a blanket and sing* ELIZABETH *a lullaby: The Shirelles' 'Dedicated to the One I Love'. Lights change throughout this – dusk, midnight, blackout.*

Scene Six

CLARA. Morning, miss.

CLARA leaves a letter. ELIZABETH *inspects it. No sign of who it's from. She looks around. The* SERVANTS *are nowhere to be seen. She slowly opens it.* DARCY *appears magically as the voice of the letter.*

ELIZABETH. Dear Elizabeth, don't be –

DARCY. – alarmed at my sending a letter. I won't mention any of my feelings that were so disgusting to you yesterday but I had to clear a few things up. I –

She hurriedly balls up the letter and throws it on the floor.

A beat.

The SERVANTS *enter. Together, they delicately pick it up, smooth it out, place it strategically so that she happens upon it again. She can't resist. She reads.*

I could see that Bingley was genuinely in love with Jane when I advised him to move back to London.

ELIZABETH. The gall.

DARCY. But that is why I did so. Jane was polite – but
    nothing more. I concluded – the feeling couldn't possibly
    have been mutual.

    And your mother boasted so openly about the certainty of
    their marriage.

ELIZABETH. Mum…

DARCY. I wondered – would Jane have even had the choice
    to decline if Bingley had proposed. And where would my
    friend be then? Married to a woman who didn't truly
    love him.

    I thought she was completely indifferent to my friend. I
    never *imagined* I'd hurt your sister.

    Now, regarding George Wickham; I don't know what
    he's told you about me.

ELIZABETH. Just the truth.

DARCY. But I will tell you everything as it happened. My
    father *was* fond of him and *did* leave him a large sum of
    money to train for a profession in the church.

    Wickham received that money in full.

    But later, he came to me asking for more. I gave him
    three times the initial amount. After that I didn't see
    him for years. Until, finally, he reappeared. He had spent
    every penny of the money he'd received on wine, women
    and gambling, and still he wanted more.

    When I refused – he severed all ties with me.

    That was the end of it, I sought no reproach. Until –
    and I trust this will stay between us – something worse
    happened. You may remember that I am guardian to my
    younger sister, Georgiana.

    Around a year ago – she would have been the same age as
    your youngest sister – she was abducted by an older man
    who persuaded her that they were in love. That man was
    George Wickham.

Had they married, he would have taken over her fortune
of forty thousand pounds. I have no doubt that money
was his motive, but perhaps also revenge against me
and... desires besides too upsetting to think of.

Luckily, I tracked them down before they could wed –
and I brought my sister home. Wickham fled, of course.
He has been avoiding me ever since.

I know your hatred of me might make these words
worthless – and you might wonder why I didn't say this
all last night... But I hope you'll understand that I wasn't
in my right mind after...

What happened between us.

I don't think there's anything else to say but –

Rest assured you'll never hear from me again.

ELIZABETH (*reading*). Fitzwilliam Darcy.

ELIZABETH *lowers the letter, astounded.*

The scene transforms.

Scene Seven

Longbourn. LYDIA*'s music plays loud, The Slits' 'Typical*
Girls'. She stomps across the space holding a brown dress.
JANE *and* ELIZABETH *sit in conference, eating cornflakes out*
of the box.

LYDIA (*with teenage fury*). Is this some kind of sick joke? How
is *this* going to help? I don't know how many times I have
to say this before you'll listen: I don't want hand-me-downs!
And I especially don't want Mary's! (*Exiting.*)

JANE. He proposed? You weren't even a little bit flattered?

ELIZABETH. Well, maybe a bit.

JANE. He is handsome.

ELIZABETH. And then that letter. To think he actually had good intentions when he split up you –

ELIZABETH *stops herself.*

JANE (*oblivious*). When he what?

ELIZABETH. Nothing.

JANE. Go on. He had good intentions when he split up…?

ELIZABETH (*thinking on her feet*). When he split up Wickham and Georgiana. He had good intentions.

JANE. Well, of course! It sounds like she was virtually kidnapped by him!

LYDIA (*from offstage*). Just leave me alone, Mum, you stupid old bitch!

ELIZABETH. They're even worse than I remember.

JANE. The militia have announced they leave Meryton in two months. For good.

ELIZABETH. Poor Lydia. About all this Wickham stuff – Darcy asked me to keep it to myself. For his sister's sake.

JANE *mimes zipping her mouth up.* MRS BENNET *cuts across the stage, after her youngest.*

MRS BENNET. The soldiers may come back next year! We could stretch to getting you a new dress, my dear, or a bonnet at least.

LYDIA. Why? No one will see me!

MRS BENNET. You can go into town every day – show it off!

LYDIA *runs off, pursued by* MRS BENNET.

JANE. Dad hasn't been able to cope with either of them. He says the longer Lydia spends in town, the better.

ELIZABETH. Of course Darcy swithered about marrying into this family. So would I…

JANE. Mary's quieter than ever, and Kitty and Lydia keep trying to cut each other's hair off in the middle of the night. Kitty nearly lost an ear.

ELIZABETH. I need to get out of here.

JANE (*thinking hard*). Erm... well Aunty G's going to the Lake District in spring.

ELIZABETH. That's not for months! Frankly, Jane, I need a holiday – and it just can't come quick enough.

ELIZABETH *looks down – the lights have changed, Longbourn and its residents are gone and the* SERVANTS *have placed a bag in her hand.*

Oh. Well, that did actually come around quite quickly.

ELIZABETH *sets off.*

Scene Eight

ELIZABETH *and* MRS GARDINER *in front of Pemberley house, in which three* SERVANTS *clean up.* ELIZABETH *is uncharacteristically unsettled.*

ELIZABETH. Pemberley? I thought we were going to the Lake District?

MRS GARDINER. What can I say? This trip seemed to come around so quickly – I ran out of time to plan. Aren't the grounds magnificent?

ELIZABETH. Well yes but... isn't this... the house Mr Darcy owns?

MRS GARDINER. Yes! It's a tourist attraction! We can go inside.

ELIZABETH (*holding* MRS GARDINER *back*). Yes...! Well – from the very little I remember about Darcy, he's not keen on surprises.

MRS GARDINER. You needn't worry. He's away.

ELIZABETH (*suddenly interested*). Away?

MRS GARDINER. Yes. He's not at home. Visiting friends in London until tomorrow. My housekeeper told me. Anyway, shall we?

ELIZABETH (*too curious to resist*). If it'll make you happy.

> ELIZABETH *rings the bell.* FLORENCE REYNOLDS, *the housekeeper of Pemberley, is there.*

FLO (*to audience*). Welcome, ladies and gentlemen, to Pemberley!

> *All at once – music in, dazzlingly beautiful lights and flowers descend.*

ELIZABETH. Oh my God…

MRS GARDINER. My, it's even grander than I remember…

FLO (*to audience*). Sixteen bedrooms…

TILLIE. Five sitting rooms…

CLARA. Three dining rooms…

TILLIE. A smoking room…

FLO. An *enormous* library – !

ELIZABETH. And the master's definitely away?

MRS GARDINER. I told you –

FLO. Ah! Tourists. Yes, I'm afraid he is away, miss. We're expecting him first thing tomorrow along with friends of his, Charles and Caroline Bingley. Now – why not start your tour here…

> *She gestures to the other* SERVANTS *to prepare their presentation of the house.*

At this window you can see the river… the trees along the bank, the winding of the valley. And in the room itself, the original fireplace – very elegant. Not to mention the focal point, an exceptional portrait of my master.

A jacket falls from the balcony, FLO *puts it on as she speaks, whirring round to appear in a frame held up by* TILLIE. *All look up at this.*

MRS GARDINER. Such a handsome portrait. I couldn't say if it was a likeness, I've not seen him since he was a little boy. I knew his father, you see. Elizabeth would know better, though. She met Darcy only recently.

FLO *spins out of the portrait and transforms back.*

FLO/TILLIE/CLARA. Oh?

ELIZABETH *is completely transfixed by the portrait.*

A couple of beats.

MRS GARDINER. Is it like him, Liz?

ELIZABETH (*softly*). Just like him.

FLO. I'd rather he were never away. I look forward to a time when he'll marry and stay more at home – but who would ever be a good-enough wife? I've not heard one cross word from the gentleman in all my years here. He's so kind, generous, caring for the poor. He's unlike any other man I know – and would probably make a very good father himself one day. Not just in my opinion, you can ask any of his servants.

The SERVANTS *make noises of agreement.*

FLO. Well, I'll leave you to have a look around. Oh! (*To the* SERVANTS.) Let them see the new harp. (*To* ELIZABETH.) Mr Darcy bought it for his sister. He's just like that... he would do anything to make her smile.

She exits.

MRS GARDINER. Laid that on a bit thick, didn't she? (*Shouting after* FLO.) Mrs Reynolds – might I see the famous library? (*Exits.*)

ELIZABETH. Aunty we need to g–

MRS GARDINER *is gone.* ELIZABETH *is left trying not to look at the portrait. The* SERVANTS *play the instrumental of 'Something Changed', as at Netherfield when they were first left alone. His eyes seem to follow her around the room.*

Darcy –

DARCY *is in the room.*

DARCY. Miss Elizabeth?

ELIZABETH. Darcy!

ELIZABETH *squeals and falls backwards over her own suitcase.*

DARCY (*urgently*). Are you okay?

ELIZABETH (*mortified but trying to act casual*). Uh-huh. You're home?

DARCY. Yes. And *you're* in my home.

CLARA. You're a day early, sir.

DARCY. I am. You're not hurt?

ELIZABETH. I'm fine.

CLARA. But you're not…

DARCY. Not?

CLARA. I mean… you're very dry, sir.

DARCY. Dry?

TILLIE. Bone dry.

DARCY. Yes. (*Baffled.*) As are all of you.

CLARA. It's as if… you haven't just emerged from a lake.

DARCY. No. I've just emerged from my carriage. Is something the matter?

CLARA. No. No, no. It's just – are you sure you wouldn't like a swim in –

DARCY. Quite sure, Hattie. Thank you.

TILLIE (*unheard by* ELIZABETH *and* DARCY). It might be sexy!

TILLIE *and* CLARA *agree not to pursue the matter.*

ELIZABETH. I didn't think you would – I understood you were away.

MRS GARDINER *re-enters.*

MRS GARDINER. It's palatial!

ELIZABETH. My aunt insisted we visit.

MRS GARDINER. Mr Darcy? An early return? What a treat. Look at you, now! So big! The last time I saw you, you were – (*Gestures.*)

DARCY. I remember – Mrs Gardiner. (*Taking her hand affectionately.*) Any true friend of my father's is like family to me.

MRS GARDINER. What an incredible home you have. And such nice servants.

The SERVANTS *silently congratulate themselves.*

They're all so complimentary about you. Elizabeth wasn't sure about coming – but I told her it was unmissable. Didn't I, Liz?

ELIZABETH. Well –

MRS GARDINER. She was worried you wouldn't want visitors. I told her – he's not in! And even if he were – the Darcys are the loveliest hosts you could meet!

ELIZABETH. Aunty –

DARCY. I'm glad you came.

ELIZABETH. You are?

DARCY. Yes. And you must let me insist that you stay the night. (*To his* SERVANTS.) I'm having some friends for drinks (*To* ELIZABETH *and* MRS GARDINER.) You must join us.

ELIZABETH. I'm not sure we can –

DARCY (*crossing downstage, speaking sincerely – his back to them*). If it's at all possible, I would be delighted to host you and your aunt, Elizabeth. It would be an honour.

ELIZABETH *in an impossible position. She looks at her aunty. This is the last thing she wants. A beat. Then a servant pops up and does a bad impersonation of* ELIZABETH.

CLARA. Well now, if you insist.

DARCY. Fantastic.

DARCY *gestures for their bags to be taken upstairs.*

MRS GARDINER. Overnight at Pemberley! Ooh – I might go to the end of the garden and back before dinner – is it walkable?

TILLIE. It's only twenty-odd miles, Mrs G!

MRS GARDINER. Twenty? That would kill me. How wonderful!

The SERVANTS *disperse –* ELIZABETH *and* DARCY *look at each other. The scene transforms.*

Scene Nine

Music, soft lighting, easy conversation. ELIZABETH *stands, is handed a generous glass of wine. She watches* DARCY *who is in the audience being incredibly charming with everyone.* ANNE *and* CLARA *carry cakes and drinks and other delicious things. It's the best drinks party ever.*

CLARA. Elizabeth had never seen him like this before.

ANNE (*to* DARCY). Microphone, sir?

DARCY. Microphone?

CLARA. When you own a house as big as yours, sir – it's prudent to use one.

DARCY. Very well.

DARCY *takes the mic and approaches the front row.*

Good evening! You all look so wonderful.

ANNE. At first she had been amazed that he even spoke to her at all – after all that had happened.

DARCY. Did you come here in that beautiful horse-drawn carriage of yours this evening?

CLARA. But for him to show such grace to her. She who had turned up at his house like this. What must he have thought she was doing?

DARCY. What was that book? You must recommend it to Miss Elizabeth – she has a very brilliant mind.

ANNE. Never had his manners been so dignified. Never had he enquired after everyone with such gentleness.

DARCY. Do you enjoy fishing? You must come here and fish any time you please. I can lend you the stuff, show you the best spots.

CLARA. She could not be untouched by his politeness.

DARCY. Are we all okay for drinks?

ANNE. Why, then, must she feel so awkward? All power of speech failed her. Every conversational topic seemed embargoed. She was so desperate to seem at ease that ease itself had deserted her entirely.

MISS BINGLEY *enters.*

CLARA. And, as ever, the presence of Caroline Bingley could only make things worse.

MISS BINGLEY. You just *happened* to be in Derbyshire? At the same time? All a bit of a coincidence, isn't it?

ELIZABETH. Sometimes... people are in Derbyshire.

MISS BINGLEY. You look pale. Are you tired?

ELIZABETH. No.

MISS BINGLEY. Would you say Elizabeth looks peculiar, Darcy?

DARCY. On the contrary.

MISS BINGLEY. Puffy. Like you're retaining water. And your eyes. Red. Shrewish. Oh – she might be rabid!

ELIZABETH. I'm… I'm fine.

MISS BINGLEY. Hmm. Perhaps that's how you normally look, then. It's been so long, I must have forgotten.

ELIZABETH. I… I, um –

DARCY. Elizabeth looks perfect. She always does.

MISS BINGLEY (*unwilling to drop it*). Are you sad, perhaps? I heard the militia have left Meryton – leaving you without your darling Mr Wickham – that'll be it! This is a sickness of the heart!

DARCY (*coolly – forcefully*). Caroline –

MISS BINGLEY. And you were so fond of him. Lovely, handsome Wickham!

DARCY. Why would I want to hear that man's name in my house?

MISS BINGLEY. I'm sorry, Darcy, I didn't mean to remind you of him and Georgiana.

ELIZABETH *and the* SERVANTS *gasp* – MISS BINGLEY*'s dug herself deeper.*

DARCY. That'll do, thanks Caroline.

MISS BINGLEY *turns to leave, grabbing a bottle of champagne as she does. Uncomfortableness for a moment. Then* DARCY *saves the situation.*

Now – coffee! I think it's time for a cup – (*To* ANNE.)

Would you be so kind?

ANNE *nods and exits*.

(*To* ELIZABETH.) If you need anything at all… just let me know. (*As he exits*.) Please make sure Miss Bennet's comfortable.

CLARA. Of course, sir.

Scene Ten

Lights up. Pemberley. ELIZABETH *wrapped in a duvet, crying and holding a letter. Three* SERVANTS *stand beside her.* DARCY *enters*.

DARCY. Good morning Eliz– My God, what's wrong?

CLARA. She's received a letter, sir.

ELIZABETH. I have to go – !

DARCY. Please. Just one moment. You're too upset.

She weakens.

ELIZABETH. It's Lydia… She…

She can't contain it. She cries, stuck to the spot.

He stands a little awkwardly. The SERVANTS *look at him imploringly.* DARCY *eventually moves to* ELIZABETH *with a handkerchief*.

CLARA. The morning after the regiment of redcoats left Meryton, The Bennet family woke up to find that Lydia was gone.

TILLIE. Run away.

ANNE. Or taken.

TILLIE. She left a letter saying only that she was –

ANNE (*as* LYDIA). '**in love with a soldier.**'

TILLIE. So there was –

ANNE (*as* LYDIA). '**no point in staying.**'

TILLIE. She was going to –

ANNE (*as* LYDIA). '**Gretna Green to marry, straight away.**'

CLARA. It was thought the pair were hiding out in some London hostelry, but no one knew which.

TILLIE. They were untraceable. And Lydia had not written since.

ELIZABETH. She's fifteen, Darcy. She has no friends down there – they have no money, they're not married, there's nothing.

CLARA. A daughter living in sin with a penniless soldier is enough to bring disgrace on an entire family – and that shame would ensure every Bennet sister remained unmarried for life.

TILLIE. Whether Lydia ended up in the family way –

ANNE. Destitute –

TILLIE. Alone –

CLARA. Or all three – would spell the end for the Bennet's reputation.

ANNE. And if the soldier had not yet married Lydia, he could fly from her whenever he chose. That's just how it works for men.

CLARA. Of course, if he did decide to marry her –

TILLIE. If we had misunderstood the situation –

CLARA. And they were merely *delaying* their wedding –

TILLIE. Then something could be salvaged for the Bennets.

ANNE. But this was unlikely because the soldier who Lydia had run away with –

TILLIE. Was George Wickham.

ELIZABETH. I had no idea she had feelings for him. But I never took a word she said seriously. She had a new favourite every week.

DARCY. You weren't to know.

CLARA. Elizabeth wondered if she could have prevented this. If she had only shared what she'd learned about Wickham with her family –

TILLIE. His gambling –

CLARA. His lying –

ANNE. His history of abducting teenage girls –

TILLIE. Then maybe Lydia would still be safe.

CLARA. All she could be certain of, as she looked into Darcy's eyes, was that whatever chance they may once have had was now gone. Forever. Her family had become a public joke. He would never propose again. And nor would anyone else.

DARCY (*he pointedly hands the letter back to her and removes himself*). I'm… so sorry.

He exits. She is distraught. The scene transforms.
ELIZABETH *has to get home.*

Scene Eleven

Longbourn. MR BENNET *in his chair as ever.* MRS BENNET, *consumed with worry, reclines, fanned by daughter* JANE.
ELIZABETH *pacing.*

MRS BENNET. Any post?!

TILLIE. No, madam.

ELIZABETH. We should have taken an interest in her, encouraged her to stay home more… told her she was bright… Do you not think?

MRS BENNET. Your father always said Lydia was stupid.

ELIZABETH. And she's proven you right, Dad. But would it not have been wise to save *some* money over the years rather than just waiting on the birth of a son…? Even at that – do you not think you should be out there now trying to find her?

MRS BENNET. No! (*To* MR BENNET.) You stay right there. If he dies fighting Wickham, we're all as good as dead!

ELIZABETH. There, there… I'm sure no one's going to die… (*To* JANE.) Maybe fetch her a glass of wine. And, Tillie – (*Gesturing to* MR BENNET.) could you –?

JANE *exits and* TILLIE *wheels* MR BENNET *off.*

MRS BENNET. All I wanted was a daughter married. To know we'd have half a chance of survival. We could offer Wickham all the savings we've got – it would never be enough. Everyone's saying he got thousands in bloody gambling debts…! In every town he's visited. The Bennets are the laughing stock of Hertfordshire! Who would touch any of you with a shitty stick, now? Oh, I can feel myself fading, Liz… tremblings… spasms in my side!

ELIZABETH. You're fine, Mum.

MRS BENNET. No, I think I'm passing over. Fetch everyone, will you? And if you ever find Lydia, tell her 'It was you who finally killed our mother, you selfish little fucker!'

ELIZABETH. Come on. Don't be ridiculous.

MRS BENNET. Goodbye, world!

ELIZABETH. Mum! For God's sake – !

TILLIE *has entered, extremely shocked.*

TILLIE. Madam!

TILLIE *stands to one side. In walks* LYDIA *in a hastily put-together wedding outfit. Plastic bouquet, tiny veil. All very cheap. Trailing behind her, mortified,* WICKHAM, *a plastic button-hole in his regimentals.*

LYDIA. Surprise!

Everyone is agog.

Mr and Mrs Wickham here to see you!

ELIZABETH. You're alive.

MRS BENNET. You're... married?

LYDIA. We are!

MRS BENNET *leaps up, completely recovered.*

MRS BENNET. Married! Our reputation's intact...? And we get to keep the house! Oh – my darling, clever girl – I never doubted you!

ELIZABETH. Mum...!

MRS BENNET. And what a handsome son-in-law!

ELIZABETH (*through gritted teeth to* MRS BENNET). Mum – his debts...! The... the abduction!

MRS BENNET. Well, he married her, didn't he? So he can't be in that much debt, we must have got it wrong. Congratulations!

LYDIA (*to* ELIZABETH). Aren't you going to congratulate me, Liz? The first one of us to get married – and the youngest!

LYDIA *kisses* WICKHAM*'s face passionately – he stands stock still.*

Don't you want to kiss your new brother, Liz?

ELIZABETH. Not especially. Wickham, what were you thinking?!

WICKHAM (*robotically*). That I loved and wanted to marry your sister, Lydia.

LYDIA. Maybe you should run away, too, Liz. Find a husband instead of moping around here all day. We're going to move to a house in Newcastle.

MRS BENNET. Newcastle?

LYDIA. You can come and visit, Mama. I dare say they have balls in Newcastle.

MRS BENNET. Balls! I love balls!

Let's have a huge party to celebrate! And buy you wedding presents! (*To* WICKHAM.) Come with me young man, you've got a lot of new sisters to kiss.

WICKHAM *stands to escape but* MRS BENNET *and* TILLIE *skilfully tackle him, one arm each so that resistance is futile.*

Silly boy, going the wrong way.

They all exit.

ELIZABETH. Come here, Lydia.

ELIZABETH *takes her sister aside. Almost against her own better judgement, she hugs her desperately. Then, talks to her as if she were quite small.*

Lydia, when you got married, did you give him any money?

LYDIA. I didn't have any money.

ELIZABETH. I know, but he's got a lot of debts.

LYDIA. Oh, those. He paid them off.

ELIZABETH. How?

LYDIA. He came into some cash. We'll live very comfortably now.

ELIZABETH. But… to clear all that debt – he would have needed an absolute fortune. So how did he 'come into some cash'?

LYDIA (*not caring at all*). He says he's very good at playing cards. Perhaps it was that. (*Enthused again.*) The wedding was *so* lovely. We travelled in Darcy's carriage and we kissed for about ten minutes straight – can you imagine, Liz?

ELIZABETH. I'd rather n– wait, whose carriage?

LYDIA. Darcy's. He escorted me to the church and signed as a witness. (*Excited again*.) So, picture the scene, the sun was shining on us as if the angels themselves had –

ELIZABETH. He signed?

LYDIA (*irritated to be interrupted again*). He signed loads of stuff! A contract thing, some cheques – (*New thought*.) Oh, wait, yeah. George did say not to mention Darcy was there. It was supposed to be this big secret or something. (*To herself*.) I swore on Mary's life, as well… Oops. You won't say that I said anything, will you, Lizzie?

ELIZABETH (*feigning ignorance*). No. 'Course I won't.

LYDIA. I did think it was a bit weird. Me hardly knowing Darcy and all…

Giggles and squeals from off.

Kitty better keep her fucking paws off my man…!

LYDIA *runs off to attack her sister.* ELIZABETH *is left alone with this information. A light in the living room flickers – then short-circuits.*

Scene Twelve

Disorientation. Darkness. Then, one second later, lights up. LADY CATHERINE DE BOURGH *is in the Bennet's living room.*

LADY CATHERINE. Elizabeth Bennet.

ELIZABETH. What the – ? Lady Catherine! You're in Meryton?

LADY CATHERINE. Yes, I am *that* unfortunate. Do you have designs on my nephew?

Beat.

Right. Cut all ties with him immediately.

ELIZABETH. You won't influence me.

LADY CATHERINE. You are receiving advice from someone vastly superior, Miss Bennet. Hear it in silence. Darcy is already engaged to my daughter, Miss de Bourgh.

ELIZABETH *is thrown*.

ELIZABETH. He proposed to her, did he?

LADY CATHERINE. He didn't need to. His mother and I made an agreement when they were children.

ELIZABETH. Congratulations. As this doesn't concern me, I'll just –

LADY CATHERINE. Any woman who sought to derail that plan would be cast out. Her name would be poison.

ELIZABETH. I think she'd probably get over it.

LADY CATHERINE (*losing her temper now*). Do you know who I am? How low you are to me? What an insignificant parasite you are to my nephew.

ELIZABETH. I doubt very much that he said that.

LADY CATHERINE. Everyone knows about your whoreish little sister's elopement, your meagre savings, your horrific mother. So if you think that I would let you pollute my family, you are grossly mistaken.

ELIZABETH. Darcy is my equal.

LADY CATHERINE. You are quite deluded. And too sharp-tongued for your own good!

ELIZABETH (*smirking*). Your nephew seems to quite like it.

Beat.

LADY CATHERINE*'s nostrils flare – she is absolutely incensed at this insolence. She just manages to keep a lid on it.*

LADY CATHERINE. I see. You are determined to drag him down to your level. Well, I won't let you. Be assured, Darcy will be married to my daughter within the fortnight and you need never bother him again.

LADY CATHERINE *leaves.* ELIZABETH *tries to laugh this off but can't.*

The lights flicker once more. Darkness.

Scene Thirteen

Lights up. The room, just as before, but MRS BENNET *asleep in her chair. As if by magic.*

JANE *enters with sherry and glasses for her sister and mother who wakes at the familiar clinking. A lethargy in everyone. The story's over.*

JANE. So that's it. Lydia in her marital home.

ELIZABETH. I swore it would be you.

JANE. Not my destiny, Liz. I have to face facts. (*Unconvincingly.*) We'll be alright.

ELIZABETH. Yeah. Lots of people live with their mothers indefinitely.

JANE. Won't do us any harm.

MRS BENNET, ELIZABETH *and* JANE *all raise their glasses to their mouths in the exact same manner to sip their sherry, before sighing in unison.*

MRS BENNET. Give us a song, Lizzie.

ELIZABETH. No. I won't be doing that.

MRS BENNET. Oh God, you sound like that dreadful Mr Darcy.

ELIZABETH. We probably owe Darcy much more than we realise.

MRS BENNET. Don't talk bollocks, Liz. Darcy wouldn't piss on you if you were on fire. Tillie, have you drawn me that bath? (*Exits.*)

JANE. What do you mean?

ELIZABETH. Something Lydia said. I've been trying to work it out. (*Despondent.*) No point, though. He's gone. He'll be planning his wedding as we speak.

JANE (*listless – topping* ELIZABETH *up*). Yeah.

ELIZABETH. Even if I did work it out, I'll never be able to thank him.

A new realisation.

Never be able to apologise.

Something worse.

Never be able to tell him how I really feel.

ELIZABETH *is utterly in love – and realises it.*

Oh God.

JANE (*concerned*). Liz…?

ELIZABETH. Oh Jane, I think I… no, I'm sure that I'm in love with –

A VOICE. Jane! Jane!

ELIZABETH (*utter disbelief*).…No?

THE VOICE. Jane!

JANE (*half to herself*). Bingley?

BINGLEY *is at the top of the auditorium.*

BINGLEY. Jane!

JANE (*to him*). Charles! You came back!

BINGLEY. What?

JANE. You came back!

BINGLEY. I came where?

DARCY. Miss Elizabeth.

DARCY *is also standing at the top.* ELIZABETH *sees him.* JANE *and* BINGLEY *move away to be alone.*

(*Gesturing to* BINGLEY *as he leaves.*) I told him everything. That I had kept him from Jane. That it was my fault.

Beat.

ELIZABETH. Darcy, I owe you such thanks...

DARCY. Do you?

ELIZABETH. You found them, didn't you? Lydia and Wickham? You paid him off. It could only have been you.

DARCY. I'm sorry. You weren't supposed to find out.

ELIZABETH. All to save my family's reputation.

DARCY. I couldn't care less about your family's reputation.

ELIZABETH. Then for what?

DARCY. For you. No one has ever brought me more joy.

She feels the impact of these words.

ELIZABETH. Lady Catherine said you were marrying –

DARCY. Fuck Lady Catherine!

Beat. Then, fast, as DARCY *runs to her –*

ELIZABETH. I'm sorry I told everyone you were a twat.

DARCY. I was behaving like a twat.

ELIZABETH. My behaviour was far worse.

DARCY. Let's not fight for that prize.

ELIZABETH. I assumed I knew the whole story. I've been doing that all my life. Darcy, I'm so indebted –

DARCY. No, Elizabeth, nothing can compare to what I owe to you.

ELIZABETH. No –

DARCY. No, you were right. I was a selfish snob, and vain – to assume you'd be flattered by me!

ELIZABETH. I was flattered. I was just too fucking stubborn to admit it. (*Freshly embarrassed.*) And when I turned up at Pemberley –

DARCY. My heart leapt.

Beat. She looks at him – amazed at what's changed.

ELIZABETH. I insulted you. I argued with you. Is that what you liked about me? My rudeness?

DARCY *smiles.*

ELIZABETH. I understand *when* this…? When exactly did we…?

DARCY. I can't remember the hour, the spot, the words, or the look that *started* it. Just that I was in the middle before I knew that I'd begun.

ANNE enters with the karaoke machine and a microphone for DARCY.

Music in – Pulp's 'Something Changed'. DARCY sings the first verse. More free now.

DARCY holds the mic up for ELIZABETH to sing.

Then, over an instrumental, he moves to get on one knee. ELIZABETH shakes her head and stops him, pulling him back up again. She then gets on her knee – takes his hand. ELIZABETH removes a ring from one of her fingers and offers it to him. He accepts. She puts the ring on his little finger and they kiss.

The lovers exit, elated. MRS BENNET's voice is heard –

MRS BENNET. **Mr Bennet! Mr Bennet! I don't believe it! We're saved!**

No thanks to you, Mary, you bloody waste of oxygen.

The lights revert to their state from the opening.

Scene Fourteen – Epilogue

CLARA, TILLIE, FLO *and* EFFIE *appear. Marigolds, mop and bucket, cloths.*

TILLIE. So, there we go.

FLO. I enjoyed that.

TILLIE. Cheers, Miss Austen!

They smile take in the space, post-show, covered in confetti, props and bits of furniture.

CLARA. Who's going to clear up all this –? / Sorry, yes. Keep forgetting.

TILLIE. / Course, aye.

FLO. / Oh, right, obviously.

EFFIE *nods.*

They tidy.

TILLIE. In case you're wondering, Elizabeth moved in with her new husband.

CLARA. Jane and Bingley moved into Netherfield.

TILLIE. Well – for about a year. Then the proximity of Mrs Bennet became a bit too much for even them –

CLARA. So they settled in a house in Derbyshire. Close to Elizabeth and Darcy.

TILLIE. That's nice, eh?

FLO. Lydia visited seldom and wrote often. Especially if Wickham needed money.

CLARA. Wickham, himself, stayed well away.

TILLIE. Kitty escaped Meryton whenever she could, but vowed never to run away with a soldier.

FLO. Funny how things work out.

New energy.

(*Declarative*.) Elizabeth Bennet and Fitzwilliam Darcy!

CLARA. Two souls who had been asking questions their whole lives had –

FLO. In each other –

CLARA. Found *every* answer.

TILLIE. Elizabeth thought herself happier, even, than Jane.

FLO. Jane smiled daily. But Elizabeth – she *laughed*.

CLARA. And we…?

Beat.

TILLIE. Keep going.

CLARA. Doing the hardest work of all, so that other folk can sit on their arses and write concertos, poetry and even great romantic novels.

TILLIE (*grabbing a cloth*). Best crack on, then!

FLO. What cannot be cured, must be endured!

CLARA. Many hands make light work!

EFFIE. A life without love is like a sunless garden where the flowers are dead!

All turn and look at her. This isn't the right tone at all.

I mean, um – eat your greens or… your bum will fall off?

FLO. Right.

CLARA (*wracking her brains*). Are we forgetting someone…?

FLO. Oh! Mrs Bennet! She was not suddenly corrected by having so many daughters married. But spending more time with Mary did force her to soften a little.

Everyone suddenly remembers MARY.

TILLIE/FLO. / – Mary!

CLARA. And Mary! – She never did marry, but that was just fine. Because love was always alive in her heart. She –

TILLIE.…Wait – where's…? (*Counting heads.*) 1, 2, 3…

One SERVANT *is missing. All the* SERVANTS *leave the stage in pursuit of* ANNE *and the* MARY *costume.*

The stage is empty. MARY *emerges.*

She spots the abandoned mic and karaoke machine on stage. No one is there to stop her.

She looks at the audience for encouragement. The lights change and the backing starts – Candi Staton's 'Young Hearts Run Free'.

MARY *sings the first two verses. Then all the* SERVANTS *run on to join her. They sing the song together.*

Blackout.

The End.